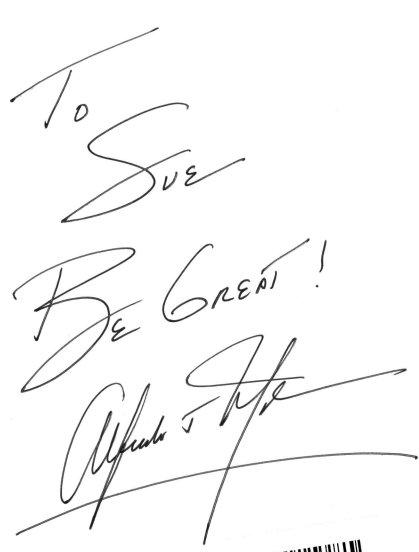

To Sue

Be Great!

Alfredo J. Tan

Be Great

TABLE OF CONTENTS

A Word from
Alfredo J. Molina

Peter H. Thomas has gone from a life of existence to a life of significance.

On his road to success, despite some serious and life-changing setbacks, Peter has always found time to give back to others.

Perhaps this generous spirit is why Peter and I have remained friends, or more like brothers, for the past two decades. We both believe that no matter how much money you make or how successful you become, life has no meaning unless you do something good with it.

In order to be great, as you will read in this book, Peter reasons that you must live life according to your values. As you will discover in the following pages, if you align your values with your priorities, your decisions will become easier to make. In turn, improved decision-making will help clear the path for you to create your own life of significance, just as Peter and others he describes in this book have. In my opinion, your path of life significance also includes sharing your values by giving back to others. As for me, that is what helps make my life a true success.

Everyone has their own inspiration for good works and where and how they pay it forward, either through donations or volunteering both in their community and worldwide. Most people choose charitable work based on a personal passion or as a result of a personal experience. My inspiration to help others stems from an unforgettable experience I had as a child, thanks to the kindness of a complete stranger.

I was born in Santa Clara, Cuba, in 1959. When I was just seven years old, the revolution forced my family to flee the grip of communist Cuba. With just the clothes on our backs, we headed to the United States as Cuban refugees and settled in Chicago.

We were taken in by the Catholic Diocese and put up in a tiny room at the Wilson Hotel, a place so rundown, dirty, and rat-infested that it was condemned and torn down just a few months after we left to more permanent housing. Upon our arrival at the Wilson Hotel, my father met a Cuban man in the lobby. That man took us to a grocery store and bought us food, which sustained our family for several days. It was the first time I had ever seen food on store shelves. It was also the first time I had ever experienced such a selfless act. To this day, I still don't know the identity of that man. He didn't ask for our thanks; he simply chose to help a family in need out of the kindness of his very big heart. That experience had a tremendous impact on me, and I believe that good deed is what has shaped my charitable lifestyle ever since.

In my professional life, I am an international jeweler, following the Molina lineage of master jewelers dating back to seventeenth century Italy. I am the owner of two retail jewelry brands: Molina Fine Jewelers in Phoenix and New York; and Black, Starr & Frost in California, which is America's first jeweler, dating back to 1810.

While I love my work and the success I have had in business to date, I could not imagine getting up every morning without also putting on my charitable hat. In addition to the retail brands, The Molina Group also includes the Molina Foundation, which supports approximately two hundred charities within the communities where I do business and beyond. My wife Lisa and our four children devote family time and many resources to the Arizona and California communities. Lisa and I have chaired numerous charity events in Arizona including the Arizona Cancer Ball, The Samaritan Foundation, The Symphony Ball, The Arizona Heart Ball, Crohns and Colitis, Women of Distinction Gala, and Childhelp, Drive the Dream. In Costa Mesa, California, we have supported Candlelite, JDRF Dream Gala, Susan G. Komen, the Pacific Symphony, Dodge College of Film and Media Arts, and we served as the honorary Chairs of the 2009 Orange Country High School for the Arts Gala. In 2005, I was honored as one of seven caring Americans, and was inducted into the Frederick Douglass Museum & Hall of Fame for Caring Americans on Capitol Hill in Washington, DC.

Lisa and I have dedicated our lives to the service of others and are proud to see our children following in our footsteps. Gratitude, selflessness, love, and a firm belief in the legacies of sharing is the foundation of the Molina way of life. Our goal has been to help improve the lives of those less fortunate. While I believe the desire to give back is a trait passed on through generations in the Molina family, alongside the craft of being a master jeweler, it was that unknown man back in Chicago who inspired me and ignited my desire to spread my generosity as widely as possible and to enhance my life significance.

The compulsion to always give back is a value I share with my good friend Peter, whose book Be Great will change your life in more ways than you can possibly imagine. Not only will it provide you the tools to help you live an extraordinary life, but this text will also help give back to others through the numerous charities Peter supports. These charities include The Todd Thomas Foundation, set up in the memory of his late son. The Todd Thomas Foundation is a nonprofit organization that helps raise awareness of the significant impact of mental illness and the effect it has on individuals, their families, and our society. Since it was founded in 2000, The Todd Thomas Foundation has raised more than $2 million and has provided funds to such community charities and foundations as the Boys and Girls Club of Greater Vancouver, the BC Children's Hospital Foundation, Young Life Canada, and many more.

Peter founded The Todd Thomas Institute for Values-Based Leadership at Royal Roads University in British Columbia, Canada. It was created to inspire leaders, organizations, communities, and nations to accomplish their highest values in action. He also founded LifePilot, an organization on which Be Great is based, that inspires positive personal change for people at any transitional stage in their life or career.

I hope Peter's wisdom and philosophies shared in this book inspire and impact your life as they have mine, so that you may live a life of significance and truly "Be Great."

Alfredo J. Molina
Phoenix, Arizona
April 2010

A Word of Introduction

*B*e *Great!* There is a very good reason why this book is not called *Be Good* or *Be Average*. It isn't in my nature to be just good or just average. It isn't in yours, either. This book will show you how to unlock your potential for greatness.

What I am about to teach you isn't a fad. The lessons you will learn here date back centuries, but of course apply to your life today, no matter what your age or the circumstances of your life. I firmly believe that everyone can have the life they want. They just need a book like this to help guide them. Cars have operating manuals, as do BlackBerry devices and even blenders, so why not humans?

What's more, you don't have to join a club or call a toll-free number for more information. All you need is a pen and a piece of paper, or laptop, your brain and this book.

If you are worried this sounds a bit too much like homework, relax. There are no tests here. There are also no deadlines. This is the beginning point of your journey to living an extraordinary life. I am willing to bet that not only will it be one of the most rewarding projects you have taken on to date, but that you will have a lot of fun doing it.

How do I qualify to pass on this information? Well, for starters, I have lived a very extraordinary life and continue to live one, now in my seventies, filled with all of the things I ever dreamed of. Today I devote my life to inspire others on how to be great, through an organization called Life Pilot (www.lifepilot.org). My colleagues at LifePilot and I have had the privilege of influencing thousands of people from all walks of life, including entrepreneurs, CEOs, employees from all sorts of companies, university students, university faculty and staff, high school students, athletic teams, military personnel, prisoners, married couples, families and others the world over.

My business background, which you will hear more about in the pages to come, includes founding and becoming the chairman of Century 21 Real Estate Canada Ltd. and turning it into one of the largest real estate networks in Canada. I also have led many significant ventures, including the development in 2000 of the Four Seasons Resort and Hotel in Scottsdale, Arizona, facilitated through my U.S. real estate company, Thomas Pride International. In addition, I founded the real estate financial services firm Samoth Capital Corporation (known today as Sterling Centrecorp Inc.) and was its chairman and CEO from 1984 to 2001. And, I put my love for music to work and invested in a Nashville-based emerging country music artist management company that handles such acts as country music star Michelle Wright.

In 2000, my life was marred by tragedy when my only son, Todd, committed suicide after a history of mental health challenges by jumping from the fourteenth floor of the New York Plaza Hotel. Since then, I have focused my grief in a positive direction by concentrating on our two charities, the Todd Thomas Foundation and the Thomas Foundation, which help raise awareness of the magnitude of mental illness and the effect it has on people and society and give funds to many other worthy causes.

A year after my son took his life I formed LifePilot, which helps empower people to reach their potential by following what I have identified as the Five Foundations. I think of these Foundations as pillars, like a support system for your life, that will help you stand tall and inspire you to realize the kind of life you thought was only for your dreams.

The Five Foundations are **values, focus, visualization, inspiration** and **reflection**. I've listed them in this order on purpose. I believe you must start your journey to a great life by first knowing what your values are, then focusing your life around those values. Once you are focused, you can visualize what you want to achieve and draw from inspirational people, places or things around you. Then, you can sit back and reflect on how far you have come, celebrate your achievements and appreciate those who have helped you along the way.

My own discovery of these foundations came in 1974, when I was thirty-six years old. I had what I can describe only as an epiphany that changed my life. It was like the skies opened up for me, and I have never looked back. What I discovered is how to clarify my personal values and align them with my goals and priorities. Sounds simple doesn't it? It can be, if you have the willpower to follow through. Many times I wished I had discovered this secret earlier in life, but it's also never too late.

In this book, I will show you how to accomplish what you set out to do, using proven methods. I will tell stories of people not that different from you who followed the Five Foundations and overcame their challenges, obstacles and fears to live the life they have always wanted, whether it was finding their ideal career, financial independence, or greater meaning through volunteerism or philanthropy. In these pages I'll share how to break free of negative patterns and habits; make decisions easily and effectively; manifest whatever you want in life; nourish your deepest longings; and put out positive energy that will help work toward attracting great things into your life.

By discovering and putting into practice the Five Foundations, you will begin to realize your full potential and your own definition of accomplishment. I wish you the greatest success in this journey—don't forget to have fun!

Peter H. Thomas
Verbier, Switzerland
May 2009

FOUNDATION 1:

VALUES

CHAPTER 1

DOING
WHAT MATTERS

Like a skyscraper that pierces a city's skyline, there is a great deal of engineering that goes into laying a solid foundation before the building begins to rise out of the ground. And, like the skyscraper, before you can reach to the sky, you must be prepared to dig deep and make your foundations strong. The most important place to start building is on your values. Your values represent what matters most to you. They affect every aspect of the way you interact with the world. What you value, you become.

This is a lesson I learned more than thirty years ago. The year was 1974, and I was attending my first Young Presidents' Organization (YPO) meeting in Hawaii. I signed up for a workshop given by Red Scott, who was then chairman and CEO of the Activa Group. I knew I could learn a lot from him. Red bounded into the classroom with a big smile, looked at the group of fifteen of us, and said, "It's far too nice outside. Let's go down to the beach." Like ducklings in a line we followed him.

At the beach, we sat around campfire-style and Red asked us a question that changed my life: "Are you living lives that honour your values?" To demonstrate what he meant, he gave each of us a pad of paper and asked us to write down what we felt our values were. We worked away for about ten minutes. Then Red asked us to list on another page all of our daily activities. That took me longer, but after about twenty minutes I had a full page. "Now, check your activities against your values," Red told us, "and see if each activity aligns with one of those values."

I compared my two lists. A sudden realization hit me smack between the eyes. Most of the activities taking up my time and energy were not related to any of my values—at least not to the degree I had anticipated.

At the time, I had listed about a dozen of my values, including being healthy, being happy, having good relationships with friends and family, and having the freedom to live and work by my own rules.

And yet, when it came to health, I realized after Red's exercise that while I considered myself healthy, I had become a work machine and was doing little to maintain a healthy lifestyle. As for relationships, I discovered that most of my relationships were work related. Anyone who fell outside of that area—sometimes even my own family—didn't see much of me. As for my family, I thought the biggest thing I could do for them was to make a lot of money and provide them

with everything they needed. What I realized was they needed more of me. I also wrote down "happiness" as a value but
realized I was trying to find most of my happiness through
successes at work and not other important parts of my life.
"Freedom," too, was on my list, which to me meant doing
whatever I wanted with my life. I thought I was free, but that
exercise helped me discover that I was in fact trapped by the
work I chose to do at the time.

I had what I call an epiphany, what the dictionary calls
"a sudden, intuitive realization." It was like being hit over the
head by a universal two-by-four, and I knew that some major
changes were in order for my life.

The philosopher Aristotle said, "We are what we repeat-
edly do." Personally and in my career I was doing okay, but
my activities were all over the place and only sporadically
aligned with my values. The exercise taught me the power of
recognizing what is important in life, and ensuring my daily
activities aligned with my values.

The results came remarkably quickly. With newfound inspiration, understanding and confidence, I left that conference in Hawaii early and flew straight to California to check
out a business opportunity. That opportunity led to the cre-
ation of real estate company Century 21 Canada, which years
later I would sell for millions of dollars. Within ninety days
of seeing Red in Hawaii, I had moved from Alberta to the
West Coast of Canada, launched Century 21 and literally
started my life over. By reaffirming my values and matching
my activities to them, I gave myself permission to change my

life. What I soon discovered is that when you live by your values, life becomes easier. Your decision-making becomes more clear-sighted, and you spend far less time wondering what you should do, how you should act, what's right and what's wrong. Your values guide the way.

From that point on, I became intent on making sure everything that came into my life was first measured against my values, which include

1. **Health.** In my life, being healthy includes doing everything from eating well and working out daily to living in and visiting places that support a healthy lifestyle.

2. **Happiness.** I am happy when I can help bring joy to everyone else in my life. When my world is happy, I am happy.

3. **Freedom.** Having the freedom to do what I want in life, both business and personal, has been key to many of my successes.

4. **Integrity.** Having integrity means maintaining my reputation as a hardworking and trustworthy person and always telling the truth, no matter how difficult at times.

Today everything I do, and I mean everything, relates to my values. If something comes along that doesn't fit into at least one of these four values I don't do it. Period.

When I go off track—which happens to everyone on occasion—my values always pull me back to what is right for my life. Not only has this mantra cleared my head for the important stuff, it has kept me alert for experiences that have the power to change my life for the better. When you live in alignment with your values, you'll experience a life filled with happiness, passion and achievement.

I believe people who are unhappy feel that way because they are not living their life in line with their values. That's because, for the unhappy people, their external world doesn't reflect what is going on inside of them. They feel inauthentic. If this sounds like you, ask yourself: "Is there a gap between the way I'm living and what I believe in?" If the answer is yes, you have to change either what you value or what you are doing. I would suggest it's healthier and easier to change what you are doing than to give away your values.

DEFINE YOUR VALUES

What are values? They are your personal principles. They define what is most important to you. Some examples of values include (but are not limited to) being successful, having financial security, having freedom to make your own choices, living a healthy lifestyle, being compassionate and generous, mentoring others, doing public service, having mutual respect for people and building wisdom.

Your values represent what matters most to you. They influence every aspect of the way you interact with the world around you.

It's also important to remember that different people have different values. These differences should be respected. There was a time when I tried to convince my wife, Rita, that our values should be the same. We had many discussions about this until I finally agreed that it made perfect sense for Rita to have her own values and for me to have mine. What's more, I opened my eyes and really explored what Rita's values were and why they were important to her. This was a real turning point in our relationship because I began to honour Rita's values, as she did mine, and we worked to align those values in our life together. Now that Rita and I know what matters most to each other our relationship is stronger than ever. We have created a true partnership. Not only does this help us to schedule and plan our lives, but also we set goals together and help each other reach those goals.

For instance, Rita really values nurturing relationships, particularly with her family, so I often organize surprises for her that relate to family and friends. For Christmas one year, I purchased tickets for her, her four sisters and her mom to go to Umberto's cooking school in Italy. We also purchased a townhouse in the Okanagan region of British Columbia, which is close to Rita's family, so we could spend more time with them.

At times we have different ideas of what we want to do, either for the day, or in making longer-term choices. When this happens, we look to our values to help us understand each other's decisions. This allows us to work in harmony. Some people find that getting in touch with their values is easy, while others have to look deeper, beneath layers of things they've invented about themselves or what other people have told them their values should be. If you are having trouble figuring out what your values are, I suggest listing ten that are the most important to you. This is key. Also remember: these are your values, not those of your spouse, your boss or your mother, but you alone. Once you've listed them, try to whittle that list down. This is how I started. Eventually, I narrowed them down to my four top values mentioned above.

WHERE DO VALUES COME FROM?

You gain your prevailing values over the course of your lifetime, and you continue to develop these values as you pass through various stages of life. Most of our values are instilled in us during our childhood, teenage years and early adulthood. Experience, role models, mentors, parents, teachers, friends and cultural icons further shape these values.

My mother influenced many of my values. We were very close. I was an only child, and I never knew my father. My mother was a strong and independent woman who loved to laugh and have fun. She was also a very positive person, and encouraged me throughout my childhood. She always gave me the feeling that I could do anything.

My mother taught me at an early age the difference between right and wrong. I remember having taken a pocketknife from the corner store as a young boy. My mother discovered it when it fell out of my pants and slid across the kitchen floor, landing right in front of her. She was so angry that I would do something like that and punished me for it, as they did in those days, with a pretty good spanking. She also made me go down to the store with her, give the knife back to the owner, and apologize. I never did anything like that again.

When I was seven years old, my mother and I moved from England to a small town in Alberta to live with a man who would become my stepfather. This was an adjustment for me. For seven years I was the apple of her eye, and suddenly she had another man in her life. I didn't like the idea that my stepfather was the provider so I decided to make my own money through odd jobs such as picking blueberries and splitting wood. As far back as I can remember I made my own money. Having my own money gave me freedom and independence, which are part of my values today.

My yearning for independence eventually led me to move to Ontario and enlist in the army at age fifteen, against my mother's wishes. For me, joining the army was a way to be free, to see the world. I wanted to go to an unfamiliar place rather than stay behind in Alberta with what was familiar. I spent seven years in the army—six at Camp Borden and one in Egypt—and believe the experience contributed greatly to my successes to date. I learned a lot in the army, including having respect for people in positions of authority even if I don't always agree with their leadership methods. I also learned the importance of discipline. Many people believe that if you are disciplined you aren't free. I believe the opposite. To me, absolute freedom is total discipline. Life is about choices. If you want to be free, you need to be disciplined to achieve it.

YOU BECOME WHAT YOU VALUE

Computers and toasters come with operating manuals. Human beings don't. Most of what we know is based on trial and error, and how much we are willing and able to learn from others. We enter the world dependent on basic needs such as food, comfort and love. As we get older, we learn to stand on our own and ride a bike and, before we know it, we're trying to balance—or even juggle—every aspect of our life.

With no operating manual to guide us, it's not surprising that so many of us wind up feeling off-balance, unfulfilled or just plain lost. We rush from one task to another. We reach for success, only to achieve it and discover it isn't as satisfying as we hoped it would be. And it seems there's never enough time for all the things that really matter to us.

When life gets complicated, I think back to an experience I had flying in a helicopter over the Whistler ski area in the coastal mountains of British Columbia. It started off as a clear day at the base of the mountain when, all of a sudden, we were surrounded by clouds so thick it was as though we were flying through milk. Life is like that. One day you are flying along quite happily and suddenly you hit rough weather, or the fog of uncertainty rolls in around you and impairs your vision. Life feels chaotic. At this point many people go out of control. Maybe your health is in jeopardy or someone you love leaves you. Or, as we've seen in recent history, maybe there's an economic downturn that puts your business or job at risk. When negative situations are thrown in front of you, it's vital to check your instruments, as our pilot did that day, and navigate your way through the storms in life. In other words, stick to your values. Knowing and understanding your values will help guide you until the rough weather calms and the fog clears.

But navigating by your values isn't just reserved for bad times. Checking in with your values regularly will give you confidence and a sense of direction at every stage of life's journey. It's easy to become lost, especially if you are in places with few discernible landmarks. Starting a new job or entering a relationship are some examples of this. If you know your values, you can use them to guide you through unfamiliar territory.

I would like to share with you a story about my friend Dru Narwani, a successful businessman and pilot who has flown his single-engine Cessna from New York to Australia. Dru has learned to navigate his own life by living according to his values and mentoring others to do the same. Years ago, Dru was at the height of a very successful banking career as the president and CEO of Standard Chartered Bank in Thailand.

At that time, he and his family were living a luxurious life in Bangkok.

But Dru felt something was missing. The answer came one evening as he sat down to dinner with his family, late as usual after a long day at the office. Even during dinner, the demands of phones and faxes meant constant interruptions. This night was no different. But for some reason, Dru paused long enough to realize his children were very subdued. "Why are you so quiet?" he asked them. They responded saying, "Mom asked us not to share things about our school because you're so busy." Dru knew this was true, but hearing it first-hand had such an impact that he immediately reassessed his values and his activities.

"I was so disconnected and so busy," Dru recalls. "My values included family, health and integrity but I had lost track of that. I said, 'It's time to follow my values.'"

Although he was still a young man, he was financially well off and decided to retire and return to Canada. Dru and his wife have journeyed far and wide in their Cessna, and have written a book about their travels.

TAP INTO YOUR VALUES

"Values are essential to living and to human happiness," said Pope John Paul II. This idea is not unique to Catholicism. It is echoed throughout the works of the world's greatest philosophers and leaders, from Socrates to Gandhi, but they didn't invent values. That knowledge has always been within us. Some of our best-known parables, fables and works of art are based on human beings' struggles to live true to their values. Even books aimed at young adults (but read by everyone), such as the Harry Potter series, contain the subtext of living true to values.

My own journey into discovering my values and living in alignment with them isn't something I invented either. I firmly believe a wise person learns from experience—and a wiser person learns from other people's experiences. As Sir Isaac Newton said, "If I have seen far, it is by standing on the shoulders of giants."

Benjamin Franklin, acknowledged as one of the Founding Fathers of the United States, understood the importance of weighing his actions against his values. He developed a list of thirteen virtues that he considered essential to his life:

1. Temperance: "Eat not to dullness; drink not to elevation."
2. Silence: "Speak not but what may benefit others or yourself; avoid trifling conversation."
3. Order: "Let all your things have their places; let each part of your business have its time."
4. Resolution: "Resolve to perform what you ought; perform without fail what you resolve."
5. Frugality: "Make no expense but to do good to others or yourself; i.e., waste nothing."

6. Industry: "Lose no time; be always employed in something useful; cut off all unnecessary actions."
7. Sincerity: "Use no hurtful deceit; think innocently and justly, and, if you speak, speak accordingly."
8. Justice: "Wrong none by doing injuries, or omitting the benefits that are your duty."
9. Moderation: "Avoid extremes; forbear resenting injuries so much as you think they deserve."
10. Cleanliness: "Tolerate no uncleanliness in body, clothes, or habitation."
11. Tranquility: "Be not disturbed at trifles, or at accidents common or unavoidable."
12. Chastity: "Rarely use venery but for health or offspring, never to dullness, weakness, or the injury of your own or another's peace or reputation."
13. Humility: "Imitate Jesus and Socrates."

Each day, Franklin checked his actions against those virtues.

Of course, which values you choose, and how many, is up to you. The goal is to create a more balanced, fulfilling life by following your own path, your own values.

To help you get started, you may wish to sign a contract with yourself—a commitment to follow your values every day, and in every part of your life.

SIGN A PERSONAL COMMITMENT CONTRACT

The power to identify and clarify your values, and live in alignment with them, generates inner peace and personal effectiveness. Committing to them enables you to discover a clear sense of purpose and direction. Here is possible wording for your personal commitment contract:

I, _____, will identify and clarify my values, and I promise to live in alignment with them in everything I do.

Date: _____
Signature: _____

Signing this contract isn't just a whimsical notion—it's a way to make your intentions clear and help you visualize living the life of your dreams. Congratulations for taking this significant step. You are embarking on a more fulfilling life. Enjoy the journey.

Share this contract with others if you like, but it's more important that you pin it above your computer or tape it to your fridge to remind yourself of your dedication to creating the life you desire.

As we'll discuss later in the book, what you visualize becomes your future.

CHAPTER 2

FIRST THINGS FIRST

You never know when your life is going to change forever. One day you're sailing along on smooth, glassy waters and life is pretty sweet; the next day a storm brews and you're tossed about, the sails torn, the ship battered, and you feel your life sinking in despair.

Sometimes you know when a storm is coming and you can prepare. Other times it hits with all the force of a tsunami, and you're left in shambles, not knowing how to pick up the pieces, or even where to begin. This happened to me on Tuesday, February 1, 2000, when I lost my only son, Todd, to suicide. He took his life by jumping from the fourteenth floor of the New York Plaza Hotel. He was just 36 years old. In the days and weeks following Todd's death, it was difficult to think of anything else, and life didn't hold much wonder for me. I felt thrust into an unfathomable nightmare. Suicide doesn't just take the life of the person who commits the act; it also takes a part of the lives of those who were close to that person.

For the first time in my life, I encountered something I couldn't fix. No matter what I could possibly do, I couldn't bring Todd back. I felt unmotivated and seemed to sleepwalk through my days without the spark, desire and excitement I always had possessed.

Then something happened that allowed me to regain touch with those things that give life true meaning. One day, at a meeting for the World Presidents' Organization (YPO), of which I am a member, a friend from Austin, Texas, Paul Robshaw, noticed the manual I was lugging around. On the cover was written *Peter Thomas' LifeManual.*

"What is that?" he wondered. I told him it was the binder from which I basically run my life.

"Do you mind if I take a look?" he asked.

"Well, it's personal stuff, but I don't mind," I replied.

Some people find it hard to grasp that I'd share such a personal item with someone so quickly, but I thought if it could help him, why not? Paul ended up making a copy of the manual so he could study it. About two months later, he called me and asked me to teach him and a few of his associates how to create their own LifeManuals.

"It's not something I teach," I explained. "It's just my own way to keep my life on track."

Paul was adamant. "We'd like to share your journey," he said.

How could I turn down a request like that? Off I went to Texas to explain the philosophy I used to guide my life. I told them about my system of ensuring everything I did aligned with my values.

As I spoke, it became apparent that everyone enjoyed the session.

Paul and I talked soon after that presentation. He suggested that I put my LifeManual into a formal training program and teach it worldwide. He felt the money I raised through the program could be given to charity in honour of Todd's life. This was a powerful, life-changing moment for me. And I made the decision that establishing a charity to honour Todd would become my main purpose, my life's work.

My priority now is to devote myself to raising funds for charitable causes in my son's name. In order to make space for this, I'm no longer looking for real estate deals, which was once my priority. This doesn't mean I won't listen to anyone who presents me with a great opportunity, but I am not actively looking. Someone can still knock, but whether I open the door or not depends on my priorities at the time.

Too many of us, and I was no different, spend time doing *second things first*. We ignore our priorities. We all need to find our "life's work"—the things in life that deserve the highest priority, and are most worthy of our time. It doesn't necessarily take a tragedy to get your priorities straight, either, but rather a passion about doing what you enjoy.

NAVIGATE BY YOUR VALUES

There is a parable about a bank that deposits $86,400 into your account every morning. This bank allows no balance to be carried over to the next day, and it offers no savings account, so whatever you don't spend wisely is lost forever. No matter how much you beg to get that money back, you can never retrieve it. If you were wise, every day of your life you would draw out every cent and spend freely. You would leave no crumbs for the bankers to reclaim. It's a great fantasy, isn't it?

But what if I told you that you really do have such a bank account in your life? It isn't filled with money—it's filled with time to spend on the things you value. Each morning, this bank deposits 86,400 seconds into your account. Each night, it reclaims whatever you failed to spend on what you value most. All of the seconds we are given every day add up to only 700,000 hours in the course of a typical lifetime.

Upon hearing this, many people feel a sense of melancholy as they ponder how much time they have let drift through their fingers. They talk about what they should have done, things they wished they'd said, and people they wished they'd treated better, forgiven or apologized to. If only they could have back some of that time. The stark truth is that there is no way to reclaim that lost time, but there is a way to start living a more meaningful, balanced life right now.

The answer is simple: spend time on what you value and weed out time-wasters that take you away from what matters most. Giving your time to what you value frees you from hours of indecision and worry, and brings you clarity of mind and purpose. You'll begin to feel a personal authenticity that many of us so easily lose as we try to change ourselves to satisfy the expectations of others.

YOUR VALUES, YOUR PRIORITIES

Once you have decided on your personal values, take some time to prioritize them. This will go a long way toward helping you achieve balance in your life. Deciding on your priorities is not a one-time task that will lead to ongoing balance. To achieve balance, you must continually adjust the weight of your values and priorities against your behaviours and actions.

How do you decide on your priorities? Here's an example: Let's say that your values are to have financial stability, to provide for and spend quality time with your family and to have independence. Which things in life deserve the highest priority? You may find that unless you find ways to honour your need for independence, you are unhappy. Yet the demands of working in a competitive corporate environment and living up to family obligations are smothering your need for independence. What do you do? First, I would ask myself, "Are there ways to attain financial freedom that complement my need for independence and still provide a source of income for my family?" Many entrepreneurs love working for themselves because it gives them a great sense of freedom. They feel like the captains of their own destinies. While it certainly has its risks, being an entrepreneur also offers the potential of uncapped income, which can contribute to greater financial stability. You are no longer locked into a monthly paycheque or the whims of an employer who may or may not value your need for freedom and your sense of family.

In terms of dealing with limitations placed on you by family, it often helps to know you'll have time to express your love of freedom. One man I know has arranged with his family to take time off twice a year by himself. During these times, he heads to the hills and hikes on his own for periods of ten days to two weeks. He returns from these trips refreshed, and his family finds he is more centred because of this solitary time, for which he has his family's full support.

Another way to successfully manage your values is to do activities that touch on as many of them as possible. One day, not too long ago, I remember being on a path overlooking the ocean. It was a beautiful day, with the sun shining and lots of families out. I stopped to enjoy the view for a few minutes and along came an interesting sight: a woman in jogging gear pushing a pram, in it a very young baby, and her husband jogging beside her with a small boy in the child carrier on his back. I could not help on that day but think that this family may have been hitting all of their values: health, happiness, family, fun, relationships, and on and on.

It may take some experimentation to get your values and activities lined up the way you want, but eventually this will become second nature to you. It might also be fun figuring out the order! As you prioritize, it may help to remember these words of wisdom by Henry David Thoreau: "The price of anything is the amount of life you are willing to pay for it."

BREAK AWAY FROM BAD HABITS

Early in life, we tend to focus on pleasing others to meet our own needs. However, as we mature, we care less about what other people think we should do and instead prefer to choose our own dreams. Breaking free of other people's expectations is often the biggest challenge. Sometimes the answer is simple but we can't see it because we're so focused on finding complicated solutions to seemingly complex problems. We've built a habit that's holding us back.

Rita and I saw this so clearly on a trip we took to Thailand. There, we had the fascinating, albeit conflicting, experience of learning how the Thai people train elephants. In this centuries-old practice (which of course many in our Western culture consider unacceptable), a young elephant is chained by one of its legs to a post. The elephant soon discovers it can only move a few feet away from the post. After two or three years of being chained, the elephant no longer needs to be tethered to the post. As long as the chain remains around his leg, the elephant will not stray or even attempt to escape. It believes, out of habit, that it is still chained to the post.

As humans, we like to think we know better than animals, but we are also tethered by our habits. All we have to do is pull away. It's so simple, but our habits often hold us back from the possibilities. We often come up with amazingly tangled reasons for not letting go of negative habits, people and situations. We have all met that person who has a job they hate, but won't leave it, or a friend who betrays them, but they continue the negative relationship that brings unhappiness into their life. Don't be that person.

The world offers every opportunity to erode your values, in big and small ways. Don't give in. Canadian sports legend Herb Capozzi once shared with me some great advice he got from his father, Pat Capozzi. He said, "Peter, never fight with a pig. You can't win. You'll just get dirty and the pig loves it." I try to remember this when I'm dealing with any issue that has the potential to drag me down.

Learning how to break away from negative patterns and habits begins with getting to know yourself better and consciously identifying what you really value.

MANAGE CHAOS

Knowing your values will help you better manage chaos—to expect it, embrace it, but not get caught up in it. The key is not to lose sight of your values. Trust that they will guide you through any situation. Losing sight of what matters is seldom a sudden occurrence; it's a process of erosion. Who hasn't heard the story of the successful business owner who started a venture in the hopes of making his family wealthy and happy, only to end up divorced and unsatisfied? Even as he told everyone that family was what he valued most, his family was slipping away from him because his reality wasn't in line with his values.

Experts believe that when we do not live in line with our values, we encounter psychological pain. Often, it's because we've gotten on the wrong track. Sometimes we just give up, perhaps because we let others impose their values on us or we choose to ignore what we know is right. Eventually we lose our direction. When you are truly in touch with your values, they tell you when to say yes, when to say no and what to do under extreme stress.

Here's an example of how my values guided me through one of the most fog-ridden times of my life. Back in the late 1970s, the North American real estate market boomed. Then, in 1981, the bottom dropped out. One minute I was on top of the world, living a jet-set lifestyle and suffering fairly heavily from what I call King Arthur's Disease—the feeling that I was invincible. The next moment everything changed; interest rates rocketed to 22 per cent and property values fell dramatically. (I will talk more about King Arthur's Disease a little later in this book.)

I was happily in the midst of delivering a workshop to the Young Presidents' Organization (YPO) in Texas when, miles away, back in Vancouver, my business partner unexpectedly announced to a hotel ballroom full of people, as well as a national TV audience, that he was bankrupt. Suddenly, my world shifted. Before my eyes, my fortune of $150 million plunged to minus $70 million. I'm sure that at that point, many people would have understood if I had gone to the nearest bar and drowned my sorrows. They also would have understood if I'd given up and said, "I guess if my partner's bankrupt, then that's the end of me, too."

I didn't do any of those things. Instead, I took a deep breath and checked in with my values. Health has long been one of my core values, so despite the chaos I found myself in, I decided to go running rather than drink myself into a stupor. I remembered back to one night in California when my business partner and I sat awake in the kitchen at 3 a.m. discussing our problems when suddenly he stood up and said, "Let's go for a run." We headed out into the warm California night and ran like two horses with the moon shining overhead. At one point, he veered off on a route through a field that he knew. I worried there might be gopher holes in the field, but I followed him anyway. As I ran, I discovered I wasn't thinking about my problems (which were enormous to be sure), but rather I was focused on the moment. I began to gain perspective and reconnect with what I valued most. When we finally got home, I fell into bed and slept until noon the next day. It was the best sleep I'd had in months. This time around, my run had just as positive an effect.

For several years it was touch and go as to whether or not I would lose everything I had earned. Frankly, I was feeling pretty sorry for myself.

When the situation was the darkest, I had a very good talk with myself and decided to evaluate where I stood. I picked up a pencil and a pad of paper and listed my assets: health, freedom, family, friendships, reputation, relationships, self-esteem, wisdom, good work ethic, success (at least up until that time!), integrity, being a mentor, being a leader, lots of love, and on and on. In fact, the only thing that I could not put on the list was *money*.

As I saw the list of all the assets I had take shape, I suddenly felt like a very lucky man. At that moment, if someone would have instructed me to give away one of my assets, I would have chosen to give away money if I'd had it. I could always make more money, I thought, but I could never regain most of the other assets once I lost them. As pastor Billy Graham once said, "When wealth is lost, nothing is lost; when health is lost, something is lost; when character is lost, all is lost."

I believe money is likely the first thing people most would give away if their values were threatened. I am reminded of a story about a millionaire businessman named Kevin who decided to give up money after a parent–teacher night at his daughter's school. All of the children at the school had drawn pictures in paint and crayon of how they had spent their summer vacation. Kevin went searching for his daughter's picture, and eventually found it. She had drawn a picture of herself and her sister playing on their swing set in the backyard with their mom. In the sky she drew a plane with the word "Dad" written on it. It became clear to him then that his values were out of balance. He decided at that moment to change his life. The next day he resigned from the company that was keeping him away from his family and causing him a great deal of stress. The experience at his daughter's school was like an epiphany that helped bring his values into sharp focus. Kevin knew he could get another job, which he soon did. What he could not regain was the precious time with his family.

Signs that your life is out of sync with your values can come in various ways. They can come quickly, in a sudden and painful revelation, or build slowly like raindrops that eventually cause a flood. These signs, no matter how they appear, point the way. All you have to do is recognize and act on them.

WHAT DO YOU REALLY VALUE?

Legendary musician Elvis Presley once said, "Values are like fingerprints. Nobody's are the same but you leave them all over everything you do."

Deciding what you value is a highly personal process. No one can do it for you. There may be values you want to have because everyone else tells you that you should have them. But are they *your* values? Can you live up to them if they aren't yours? Do you listen to your heart, or to those who may want you to ignore your values in favour of theirs?

Many people discover themselves by rebelling against the values their parents and others try to instill in them. "I wouldn't [have turned] out the way I did if I didn't have the old-fashioned values to rebel against," entertainer Madonna once said. You may not agree with Madonna's values but the fact is that most generations rebel against the values of previous generations. It's a natural and important part of discovering who we are, a way of testing the waters, as I did when I joined the army against my mother's wishes. As we grow older and learn more, we may eventually incorporate some of these values back into our lives if we find they are right for us.

Once you identify your personal values and begin consciously living by them, they will guide you through every decision you make in your life and bring you peace of mind. If you aren't sure what you truly value—perhaps you feel lost, alienated or that something is missing in your life—look deep. You may be craving a strong connection with your values and you will benefit from identifying them and valuing them. I think the following poem sums it up:

> To realize the value of ten years: Ask a newly divorced couple.
> To realize the value of four years: Ask a graduate.
> To realize the value of one year: Ask a student who has failed a final exam.
> To realize the value of nine months: Ask a mother who gave birth to a stillborn.
> To realize the value of one month: Ask a mother who has given birth to a premature baby.
> To realize the value of one week: Ask an editor of a weekly newspaper.
> To realize the value of one hour: Ask the lovers who are waiting to meet.
> To realize the value of one minute: Ask a person who has missed the train, bus or plane.
> To realize the value of one second: Ask a person who has survived an accident.
> To realize the value of one millisecond: Ask the person who has won a silver medal in the Olympics.
> Time waits for no one. Treasure every moment you have.
>
> —Author unknown

This poem takes us back to the story of the bank that deposits 86,400 seconds into your account each day. Ask yourself again: how will I spend those seconds before the bank tries to reclaim the ones I have neglected to spend on what I value?

The lesson in this is to enjoy your life every day—don't save up to have a great time later or when you retire, and don't blow it all on any one thing. Remember the old adage that it's the journey that matters most, not the destination.

CHAPTER 3

WHY SOME PEOPLE GET ALL THE BREAKS

I've always been interested in what makes people successful. What traits or attributes do they possess that help them reach their full potential? During my Century 21 years, I observed that 20 per cent of the realtors racked up the most sales. I decided to ask them what they felt the most successful people they knew had in common. These three attributes emerged:

1. **Attitude:** Top performers have a very positive, can-do attitude. You put your attitude on every morning the same way you put your clothes on. If it is raining when you get up, are you going to let that change your day? Or are you going to focus on the things that count?

2. **Motivation:** Top performers are self-motivated. Whenever I consider a new project, I consider both my attitude toward it and my motivation to make it successful. If they aren't that strong—if I feel more strongly about another one—I pass on it.

3. **Commitment:** Top performers make commitments and keep them. Once I met a marketer for a company that made premium pet food. Its products were twice as expensive as any of the other brands. I asked him how he managed to get twice the money that other manufacturers got. He started telling me how wonderful the product was—so wonderful that at sales meetings, the president would stand up in front of everyone and eat the cat food. "Not only that," he said, "but we all eat it too. The scientists, the doctors—everyone tastes it." What that company was doing was instilling commitment in its employees.

These three character traits resonated with me. I call them my AMCs, and I have used them for years to recruit, advise and mentor people. I also believe that when you can get your AMCs in order, you will succeed in whatever you want to do. Here's more about how the AMCs can work on your life.

OPTIMISTS WIN

For most people, it's easy to maintain a great attitude when things are going well. It's more challenging to stay positive when things aren't. That is when the great attitude really needs to kick in. Martin Luther King once said that "The ultimate measure of a man is not where he stands in moments of comfort and convenience, but where he stands at times of challenge and controversy."

How we handle life when the chips are down also determines other people's attitudes toward us. Tennis champion Chris Evert was ranked number one for seven years and won eighteen Grand Slam titles, including three Wimbledons, seven French Opens, two Australian Opens and six U.S. Opens. Win or lose, she is always remembered as a favourite for her positive attitude. When asked about her winning attitude, Evert said that "If you can react the same way to winning and losing, that's a big accomplishment. That quality is important because it stays with you the rest of your life, and there's going to be a life after tennis that's a lot longer than your tennis life."

We've all known people who always find something to complain about. Think about how it feels when you are around them, or when you are the one doing the complaining. It drains the energy you need to change your circumstances.

"Complaining advertises your fears while keeping you stuck in the complaint," says Rhona Britten, the author of *Fearless Living*. Instead of giving in to the impulse to react and complain, focus on putting out positive energy to attract good things into your life. People will respond to that energy. They will admire your willingness to improve your circumstances.

To show you what I mean, I would like to share the story of a man named Bill who had trouble finding work. Bill finally got a job—as a garbage man. On his first day on the job, the boss gave him a written list of the addresses he had to go to pick up garbage. Bill looked at the list despondently. "I can't read," he confessed to his boss. "Well," said the boss, "if you can't read then you can't be a garbage man." He felt sorry for Bill so he handed him some bananas and wished him good luck. Bill went to the park to sit and think about his life. He set the bananas on the bench beside him. A man came along and asked Bill if he would sell him a banana for five cents. Bill sold him a banana.

Thinking about what happened, Bill placed the rest of the bananas on the bench in a more noticeable position. Before an hour had passed, he had sold all of his bananas. In fact, the demand was so high he figured he could raise the price to 10 cents for the last two bananas. Sure enough, they sold. Bill decided to go down to the grocery store and buy as many bananas as he could with the money from his sales. Back to the park bench he went. Every day throughout the summer, he went to the park and sold bananas. Then he started to sell different fruits, and soon he found a place for himself at the gate of the park. Bill made more and more money.

Twenty years passed, and he found himself in the boardroom of a major company to which he was selling his business, which had now grown to be one of the biggest food distribution companies in the United States. His company was worth hundreds of millions of dollars. Finally, the documents were ready to sign. The lawyers put them in front of Bill for him to read over.

"I can't read," Bill said, and he slid the documents over to his lawyer. The purchaser couldn't believe his ears.

"This is unbelievable," the purchaser said to Bill. "Here you are, so successful, without being able to read. Just imagine what you could have been if you could read."

Bill thought about it for a minute. "Yes, I know what I could have been," he replied. "I could have been a garbage man."

People with winning attitudes don't focus on what they don't have or what they can't do. They concentrate on what they have and what they can do. Don't spend your life wishing you had a better education or that you were taller, smarter or better looking. Be thankful for what you do have and get on with living.

CHOOSE YOUR OWN PATH

Too often we accept a situation as though it is our "lot in life." We feel we are powerless to make choices. A generation or two ago, most men did what their fathers did and most women did what society expected of them. Today, thankfully, most of us have rejected the notion that we live predetermined lives. We can choose our own path, using the qualities we've been given.

A great example of this can be found in a story told by inspirational writer Norman Vincent Peale. He once met two brothers: one was an alcoholic and the other was a teetotaler. He asked the alcoholic brother why he was an alcoholic and the brother answered, "Because my dad was an alcoholic." He then asked the other brother, "Why are you a teetotaller?" He answered, "Because my dad was an alcoholic."

You don't have to become what other people think of you. It can be very difficult to pursue your own choices, especially if powerful forces such as family or peers are working against you, but the rewards are worth it.

DON'T FEAR FORGIVENESS

During my career, I've had many instances in which I could have fed my anger, acted vengefully and refused to forgive the actions of others, but I've learned that when you can't let go and forgive, it's a total waste of your time and the person who suffers most is you.

Giving energy to something is like feeding it. Some people might ask how is it possible to feed forgiveness and not anger. I look to people like Desmond Tutu, who won the Nobel Peace Prize in 1984 for his work to end apartheid and create a just Africa. After all the cruelty he endured, he still found it within himself to forgive. "I must forgive," he explained, "so that my desire for revenge does not corrode my being."

Mother Teresa once wrote a poem that I think sums up the power of a positive attitude, perseverance and the will to forgive:

People are often unreasonable, illogical, and self-centered
Forgive them anyway
If you are kind, people may accuse you of selfish, ulterior
  motives
Be kind anyway
If you are successful, you will win some false friends and
  some true enemies
Succeed anyway
If you are honest and frank, people may cheat you
Be honest and frank anyway
What you spend years building, someone could destroy
  overnight
Build anyway
If you find serenity and happiness, others may be jealous

Be happy anyway
The good you do today, people will often forget tomorrow
Do good anyway
If you give the world the best you have, it may never be enough
Give the world the best you've got anyway.

DO IT FIRST, THEN YOU'LL FEEL LIKE DOING IT

During my early days of selling mutual funds I took the Dale Carnegie self-improvement course, in which the trainers teach you that if your spirits are low and you need motivation, you should do the following exercise: Place both your hands in front of you, make a fist and clasp the other hand over it. Then shake your joined hands vigorously from side to side at the same time loudly proclaiming over and over "Act enthusiastic and you will be enthusiastic."

Some time after taking the course, I went out on a late-night sales call. To say I didn't feel like doing a sales presentation at 9 p.m. in the middle of the Canadian winter would be the understatement of the year, but I went anyway.

I was standing outside the door of the apartment, but still in no mood to give a presentation. Then I remembered the Dale Carnegie exercise. If I ever needed something to boost my motivation, it was then. I knocked on the door and didn't hear any sound inside the apartment, so I set down my briefcase and started to do my exercise, quietly mouthing the words "act enthusiastic and you will be enthusiastic" and vigorously shaking my arms side to side. It actually felt pretty good. Soon, I began to really feel recharged. Then I turned around to see two people standing in front of the apartment that was directly behind me, laughing. What's more, the people with whom I had the appointment were visiting with them. Embarrassed, I explained about my need for motivation and the Dale Carnegie exercise. They laughed and I was invited to give my presentation to all of them. I made four sales that night. Since then, I fully believe how we act definitely influences how we feel.

BEWARE OF KING ARTHUR'S DISEASE

When you have a hard time staying positive, consider whether or not you are carrying the baggage of negative or detrimental attitudes. You may need to cast off these weights to stay in the air and really soar. This was a lesson I had to learn a number of years ago—and I've never forgotten it.

After several years in business, I began to realize some success. My confidence as well as my professional profile grew. Soon, other business people sought my advice and asked me to speak to various organizations about how I had managed to become successful. I told them the country was going through a great growth period and that I was lucky to be in a business and a niche where I could take advantage of that growth. Lots of people just smiled and reminded me that, while what I said was true, other people were not making it and I was truly wise and special. It was very difficult not to agree with them as they fed directly into my ego. Inside, I think I did agree with them—if not wholeheartedly, then pretty substantially.

As I continued on my upward path, my attitude began to change from good to overconfident. More and more deals were offered to me, yet I sought advice less and less. Previously, I had always consulted my lawyers, my accountants, my wife and generally anyone else I thought could give me input. I felt I didn't need that advice anymore. After all, who was really making all of these brilliant decisions? Some of these deals were remarkably successful. Even when the deals went bad, thankfully I had structured exit strategies so I didn't get burned too badly.

With so many wins, I opened myself up to anyone who wanted to talk to me about a new deal. I became a deal junkie or, as they sometimes say in kinder tones, "a serial entrepreneur." Sure enough, like 99 per cent of the people on this type of path to destruction, the deal that can "kill" you is just around the corner. It did come and it was a miracle that it didn't bankrupt me.

When things slowed down a little, I had time to reflect and ask myself, "What happened?" I realized how far I had strayed from the early business principles that, in fact, had made me successful. In studying a lot of businesses that ended in bankruptcy and lives that were shattered, I began to recognize a definite pattern. In fact, I saw it so many times that I felt I should give this malady a name so others could also recognize the symptoms. I call this malady King Arthur's Disease. The disease applies equally to men and women. The unfortunate victim feels as invincible as King Arthur; nothing can destroy him. He feels he can continue to go into battle (business) just like King Arthur and come out victorious. Well, we all know what happened to Camelot in the end.

If you are a successful Type A personality, you are particularly susceptible to developing King Arthur's Disease. This disease is as dangerous to your career as it was to King Arthur, who rushed into battle without armour, against a foe he knew nothing about, because he had not done his research. Foolhardy, to be sure. Fortunately, I overcame King Arthur's Disease by checking in with my values and putting my life into perspective.

STICK WITH IT

We've talked about the importance of having a positive attitude, as well as getting and staying motivated to reach your dreams. But beyond that you need to stay committed to your dreams, especially when the going gets tough.

We talked about the pet food people who ate their own product. That's commitment. I also love the story about George Edward Arcaro, one of the most famous jockeys in history, whom *Sports Illustrated* once called "the most famous man to ride a horse since Paul Revere." Eddie, as he was known to millions of fans, won 4,770 races during his thirty-year career. He was one of only two jockeys to win the Kentucky Derby five times, and the only jockey to win the Triple Crown twice. Eddie was the leading money winner three times. By the time he retired in 1962, he had won 549 stakes races and more than $30 million—both of these were records. What most people overlook about Eddie's extraordinary career is that he actually *lost 250 races in a row* before he ever rode a winner to victory.

It's easy to become discouraged when the path to our goals isn't a straight runway to success. But many successful people will tell you their character was built as much by their so-called failures as their successes. So stick to it, and stay positive!

CHAPTER 4

WHEN TO SAY YES, WHEN TO SAY NO

Early in life, I saw the power of standing up for myself and of making good choices, beginning with my decision as a young boy to join the army. When you're that young, it's sometimes easy to get swayed from what you know is right.

My value judgment was put to the test after I finished basic training and was allowed to have weekend and evening passes. Those passes gave me a lot of freedom. Looking for something to do one night, my friends and I piled into a car and roamed the city. All of a sudden, the driver and the guy in the front seat stopped the car on a city street and jumped out. That's when things really got out of control. There was an ear-piercing screech; it was the sound of metal. I looked out the window. My buddies were stealing hubcaps from a parked car. My conscience began to play a movie of me being hauled off to jail and booted out of the army. I grabbed the car door handle, thrust the door open, and jumped out of the car. I ran as fast as I could away from there and eventually caught a bus back to the base.

At that point, I made a choice. I didn't have long to ponder which path to choose—right or wrong—or how to choose. In the blink of an eye, I drew on what I knew to be right and wrong, and chose to get out of there.

Every day we are faced with a myriad of choices. What constitutes a right choice and how do you know if you are making one? A right choice is a decision you make because your values tell you it's the right option for you.

THE POWER OF CHOICE

One of life's greatest gifts comes when we realize we have the power to make our own choices and therefore direct our lives. The idea that you can control what happens to you is liberating, yet at the same time, it can be a powerfully frightening experience because with choice comes responsibility. The path to happiness, fulfillment and success is about making your own choices and being accountable for them.

If you are having difficulty making a decision, remember to stay true to your values, then make a choice. Remember too that you are accountable for your choices. They are not something that you can switch on and off at will. They are a part of you. As I've said, and will continue to reiterate, *when you values are clear, decisions become easier.*

We are faced with many, many choices throughout our lives, and how you view and manage choices is the key to your ability to live a fulfilling and balanced life. Here are some important questions to ask yourself:

- Do you see yourself as a person with the capacity to make choices?
- Do you exercise your power to choose, or do you wait for choice to be bestowed on you by people you feel are more powerful?
- Do you see so many choices that you feel overwhelmed?

It's amazing how many people feel they do not have choices or the right to make their own choices. Sure, they may feel they can choose in small areas of their lives, but what about choosing their destinies? It's a nice dream, they'll tell you, but that's all it is. For these people, life just happens.

Many years ago I published "Passport to Business Success," an inspirational booklet that looked a lot like an actual passport. I handed it out to friends and associates, many of whom said they were inspired by the following passage: "There are people who have what it takes to make it happen; there are people who worked very hard to make it happen; and there are people who say, 'What happened?' People who consciously make choices never have to ask, 'What happened?'"

Choice is everywhere. Sometimes you'll make the right choice; sometimes you'll make the wrong choice and be forced to learn from your mistakes. But to simply accept what life throws at you and not become conscious of your options is like always driving your car through a snowstorm on cruise control. Sure, you might make it through unscathed, but you will learn nothing about how to handle the situation. You could also crash. Either way, you are not making any choice on how to steer your own course.

OPEN YOUR LIFE TO CHOICE

I'd like to open your eyes to the power of choice. To begin, take a moment to do a small exercise. Say to yourself, "I have choices." Can you feel how powerful that is? Try it again. "I have choices." You may not believe it right away, but the more often you say it, and act on it, the better you'll become at making choices and following them through to your dreams. Every choice moves us closer to or further away from something. Where are your choices taking your life? What does your behaviour demonstrate?

The biggest and most important choice you can make in life is about your attitude. Remember the AMCs—attitude, motivation and commitment? There are many things in life you can't control, but you can choose how you will respond to life's circumstances. When my son Todd died, there were many routes I could have chosen. No one would have blamed me if I had withdrawn from the world, but because I'm a positive person, I chose to honour and celebrate my son's life by creating the LifePilot organization, which empowers people to live in alignment with their values. This choice has spirited me into a new mission in life, and has put me in touch with people worldwide who are craving the tools to make positive choices.

CERTAINTY IS SELDOM CERTAIN

How do you know which route to travel? How do you decide which choice to make? The truth is, there's no way to be 100 per cent certain. However, I've discovered that living by my values has helped me make many choices that, looking back, were wise ones. Think of some choices you're grappling with and ponder them in the context of your values. Just as your values will help you decide which road to take, they can also tell you when to stop and take a different route.

Cheryl Wheeler is a painter in Vancouver, but for years she ignored that passion. Instead, she pursued a business degree and eventually became president of a publicly traded company. A few years ago, she and her partners decided to sell the company, which presented Cheryl with what she calls "an important fork in the road—a moment that I sensed would leave me forever changed." Would she stay in the business world and continue to work at a career she spent twenty years building, or finally follow her passion to paint? "It was a question of truth and faith," she recalls. "Did I have the courage and strength to let go of that which was financially rewarding but emotionally empty?"

In the end, she made the choice to pursue her passion to paint, a decision that was supported by her husband. She went to art school and not long after started to sell her own work. These days, she paints in Vancouver and Mexico.

"Today I am not who I once was," Cheryl says. "I have gained peace and serenity in my life. I pursue my passion each day with vigour and grace. When I begin a new painting I am briefly apprehensive, but life's beauty, love and energy begins to flow through me. I am inspired. I feel blessed. I experience small miracles with each new day and each new brush stroke."

It wasn't a choice most people would consider easy, but the amazing thing about choices is that when they are right, opportunity seems to flow out of them.

Fortunately, Cheryl has the support of a loving family, friends, mentors and teachers who encourage her to live her dreams. Hopefully, you have this kind of support network, but if you don't, you may have to build a network of people who will encourage and support you. (We'll talk more about mentors and surrounding yourself with supportive people later in this book.)

Another painter, Georgia O'Keeffe, made a similar choice at one point in her life. Feeling locked in by the demands of others, she said, "I can't live where I want to. I can't even say what I want to! I decided I was a very stupid fool not to at least paint as I wanted to." With that choice, Georgia O'Keeffe became one of the most celebrated artists of the twentieth century. She also began to live where she wanted to, in the desert of New Mexico, and she certainly said whatever she wanted to. She became known for her biting wit and outspoken brilliance. "I've learned, the hard way," she shared, "that some poems don't rhyme, and some stories don't have a clear beginning, middle, and end. Life is about not knowing, having to change, taking the moment, and making the best of it, without knowing what's going to happen next."

STAND UP FOR YOUR LIFE

Sometimes, you can be your own worst enemy when it comes to making choices. After all, it's easy to wallow in self-defeating thoughts instead of focusing on the positive aspects of choice. You might expect others to be angry about your choices. You might worry about disappointing people. You might feel small in the face of opposition, or too embarrassed to make waves. But all you have to do is go to your favourite video store to find real-life stories of everyday people from Erin Brockovich to Muhammad Ali and dozens of others who stood up for what they believed in and overcame huge hurdles to achieve their goals.

When I was having my financial troubles back in the early eighties, my life became a blur of meetings. At one particularly tough meeting, I faced a group that had given us $25 million.

It was invested in various real estate projects all over North America. They were panicking and demanding their money— immediately. Needless to say, this was impossible. It took six months, but finally we were able to arrange a meeting of all the parties involved. I hoped at that meeting to work out fair repayment terms. I arrived at the meeting at the appointed time with my lawyer and my accountant. There were about twenty-five people in the room, including bankers, lawyers, accountants and others. I recognized one of the men and I smiled at him. He looked back at me and, without even smiling, said, "Did you bring the money?" I stammered a bit and said I didn't think that was an appropriate way to begin our meeting. "Does that mean you didn't bring the money?" he replied.

I stood there for a few seconds looking at him before turning around and marching out of the room. My lawyer and accountant followed me to the elevator and asked what I planned to do. "The one thing I'm not going to do is sit in that room and be insulted," I said. I told my lawyer to go back and announce that, when the group decided to be civil, we would be pleased to reconvene a meeting, but there would be no meeting that day.

It actually took about two months to set up another meeting. I sent my lawyer and my accountant but I did not attend. At the end of the day, we settled satisfactorily, not only with this loan group but with all of the people to whom I owed money. I never did have to declare bankruptcy, which was important to me. However, what was also important was that

I demanded to be treated with integrity, which is in line with my values. No matter how bad things look or get, never give up your dignity or your integrity. Everyone gets into trouble at one time or another and everyone deserves to be treated with respect.

When you make choices based on your values, you'll find that making the right decisions is easier than you expected. You won't feel compromised or uncertain because everything you do, every choice you make, will be within the goalposts of your values. How can it be misguided to say no to a risky investment if financial stability is what you value most? How can it be wrong to say no to joining a 7 a.m. business gathering if your daily morning jog is a vital part of valuing your health? By knowing and abiding by your values, you'll begin to live by your own agenda instead of the agendas of others. You'll also begin to understand how it is really you—and not the people around you—who limit your choices the most. Again, your attitude will determine your options. Keep your attitude positive and your options will open.

BEWARE SNAKES AND DEVILS

Have you ever pictured a devil on one of your shoulders and an angel on the other, just like in a cartoon? Usually they are pressing you to make a choice. When in doubt, follow your values straight to your conscience. In this way, you won't be forced to live with regret. Always make the decision that you know in your heart is the correct one and never knowingly allow others to put you in jeopardy.

Many years ago, I read a fable about a little girl who was walking down a garden path when she noticed a small snake lying directly in front of her. As she reached down to touch the snake, it spoke to her. It said, "I am a snake. If you pick me up I will probably bite you, but I'm very cold and would like you to pick me up." The girl ignored the snake's warning. She picked it up and held it until it got warm. The snake then bit the little girl hard on the hand and she started to cry. "Why are you crying, little girl?" the snake asked. "You knew perfectly well what I was when you picked me up and I warned you what I would do. I'm a snake. I can't help it. You should have known better than to trust me."

Many times in your life you'll encounter snakes. If you choose to "play" with them, you will get bitten. Often, when you look back you'll realize that all of the warning signs were there. Sometimes, it's easy to ignore the signs because the snake is so well clothed, or so well mannered, or seems to hold power over you, but as an Indian proverb says, "The cobra will bite you whether you call it cobra or Mr. Cobra."

I learned first-hand about the power of snakes during my early days in real estate. At one point, when the market was down, my interest was piqued by a call I received from an acquaintance asking if I would be interested in hearing about a proposal to set up a lending office in the area. I said I was interested, and didn't hear from him again until the phone rang one Sunday at 9 a.m. I was asked to show up at a meeting later that morning to meet his associates. I went, thinking it could lead to an extraordinary business opportunity.

I arrived at the hotel at the specified time, went up the elevator and knocked on the door of the room. Inside the room were three men. We said our hellos, then one of the men walked over to the dresser and turned on a tape recorder. "Listen to this," he told me. What I heard were the sounds of gunfire, people screaming and engines roaring.

The man then shut off the tape recorder and asked me what I heard.

"I heard a lot of noise," I answered cautiously and a bit confused. "This is what we do," he said. I still didn't understand. "What did you hear?" he asked again. I was actually getting a little tired of the game. "I don't know," I told him. Then he threw me the punch line. "We finance wars." The room went silent. I still couldn't understand what he was driving at.

He went over to a drawer, took out a roll of bills and tossed them to me. "What's that?" he asked me. I looked at the roll of money and said, "It's a roll of American one hundred dollar bills." "Look at it again," he told me. I looked again and he asked me once more, "What do you see?" I still saw a roll of $100 bills. "Look carefully at the serial numbers on the bills," he ordered me.

As I thumbed through the bills it all became clear—the numbers were all the same. These guys were counterfeiters and they thought I would be a good guy to launder their counterfeit money—that I'd be a willing confederate because of my precarious financial position with the market being down.

I began to sweat. How I could get out of there? Would these guys kill me if I didn't do what they wanted? What should I do next? My mind raced, but my body felt disconnected and numb. I looked up at the three men and said, "Oh yeah, I now understand what you do. I don't think I'll be able to help you."

I jumped up and headed for the door before any of them could move. I grabbed the doorknob, twisted it and pulled hard. Thank God the door opened. I sprang into the hall, ran to the elevator, pushed the button and stood there for about one second before I dove frantically for the stairs. I raced down to the lobby and out to my car.

As I started to drive home, I wondered if they would find me and kill me. What should I do now? I called my lawyer and luckily he was at home. He told me not to panic, and predicted they would not try to contact me. We considered the options and decided there was no point in contacting the police because I didn't have any information on the men, not even a phone number for my "friend," the original contact.

I never heard from any of those dubious characters again. One day, about a year later, I saw the fellow who had asked me to meet them. He never said a word—he just disappeared as soon as he saw me.

No matter what situation you find yourself in, remember that you alone control your destiny by your power of choice. No matter what opportunities come your way, they must be measured against your values. When I look back now, I see that making a different decision at any of those critical points could have changed my life, and not likely for the better. Life is full of temptations. Some are worth indulging, but I would say only if they are aligned with your values. For me, there was no question of what was the right thing to do in that hotel room. Because I knew what my values were, the choice was easy.

GETTING PAST THE GREY AREAS

Life gains clarity when we know and live by our values, but even then we may encounter grey areas. Early in my management career, I gained some wisdom about how to handle these situations. I was in a sales contest between all the regions of the mutual fund company where I worked. As the youngest and probably the most aggressive new branch manager, I wanted my team to win. In the last week of the contest, I found out that two other branches were running neck-and-neck with our branch. We had to pull ahead. We drew up a strategy to head out to any territory in the province in that final week where we felt we could get sales.

Five days later, all my team members had made sales, but as I went through their paperwork I found that two of them had written up most of their sales in a neighbouring province. We weren't licensed to sell beyond provincial boundaries. These sales definitely would have put us over the top and we would have won the contest, but was it right if the sales were out of the province? The salespeople reasoned that the out-of-province sales qualified because even though the purchasers lived out of province, their post office boxes were in the province in which we were licensed to sell. They even bought their groceries in our province, I was told. In all ways except their actual residences, they were qualified to buy the mutual funds we were selling. Sure, the lines were a little blurred, but my sales team had a good point. As their manager, should I accept the sales or not?

Whenever grey areas come up and I can't quite figure out what to do, I turn for advice to my mentors or other people I admire. This time I felt that the situation was so specific that the only person who could help me was the president of the company. He listened, then paused and said, "Peter, where did the individuals your salespeople sold the mutual funds to actually live?"

"They actually live in the adjoining province but..." He cut me off.

"What province are these salespeople licensed to sell in?" he asked.

"In this province," I answered.

"So what's your question?" he asked.

The answer was so obvious I actually felt ashamed for seeking his advice. I thanked him for his time and turned to leave. This is when he gave me one of the best pieces of advice I've every received in my life, and one that I always think of when there are grey decisions to make.

He said most questions have simple answers if you think of the situation in black and white. "They only get complicated when you think of them in grey."

RELY ON YOUR VALUES TO POINT THE WAY

Up to this point I have tried to show you just how important it is to define and then stick to your values. Your values will help shape you. And, as I've said, once you define your values, your decisions will become easier to make.

Let me finish this chapter by telling you another story from my army days, when I was forced to make a quick decision that could have changed the course of my life. I was seventeen years old and had a ten-day leave from the base in Ontario where I was stationed. My plan was to drive to Alberta to visit my family. I didn't have a lot of cash, so when a friend of mine said he knew someone whose brother needed a ride, and could help pay expenses, I happily agreed.

We met on the day of the trip and began our journey. The boy was about fifteen years old and seemed like a great kid. Our first stop was at a gas station along the highway. I went to the pump, filled the tank with gas, paid the attendant and returned to the car. My fellow passenger was missing so I sat for a while and waited.

After about five minutes he came racing back to the car, jumped in and said, "Let's go." I didn't think much of it and drove away. A few kilometres down the road, my new friend pulled a few handfuls of paper money out of his pocket and threw it on the seat between us. "Now we don't have to worry about expenses," he said, laughing.

It took about a minute for me to realize that he had robbed the gas station. I felt a pull in my stomach and thoughts of prison flashed in my mind. I could see no way that I wouldn't be implicated if we were caught. Suddenly I knew what to do. I slammed on the brakes, almost throwing my passenger through the windshield. When the car stopped, I leaned over him, opened the door and pushed him out onto the side of the road. I threw all of the money he had stolen out with him. I then hit the gas pedal and sped away. I drove as fast as the car could go for about a half an hour, keeping one eye on the road and the other on the rear-view mirror to see if the police were chasing me. I never heard from my "friend" again and I never heard from the police.

When I look back at that story, and the others I've shared with you in this chapter about making quick decisions in difficult situations, I am thankful that I had my values to guide me. The key message I'd like to leave you with here is always to make the decision that you know in your heart is the correct one and never knowingly allow others to put you in jeopardy.

FOUNDATION 2:

FOCUS

CHAPTER 5

WORK MAGIC
IN YOUR LIFE

I like the old German proverb that says, "The main thing is keeping the main thing the main thing." This is valuable advice regarding the second foundation for creating an extraordinary life: focus. A lot of things seem to happen for me, and it's not because I'm luckier or more worthy than other people; it's because I've learned how to focus. I'm a big believer in the magic of focus—that whatever you focus on, you bring about by having a plan of action and sticking to it. If you want something to happen in your life, you must concentrate on it and take the steps necessary to make it your reality. Let me tell you a story.

When I was twenty-four, I went to work selling mutual funds at First Investors Corporation in Edmonton. At that time, many of the company's salespeople used to go to a coffee shop each morning. It was kind of an honour to be asked to join them, so when invited, I went along. I did this for about a month and had fun, but I silently wondered about all the time this wasted. Most of the salespeople would head to the coffee shop around 10 a.m. and stay until 11:30 a.m. Then they would head back to the office to check their messages before taking off for lunch.

One morning I stayed at the office to finish some work while the others went for coffee. I completed my task and was about to leave for the coffee shop when I glanced over my shoulder, and saw the number-one sales guy in the office, Don Slater, sitting in his office. I knocked on his door.

"Would you like to join us for coffee?" I asked him.

"Why would I go there?" he replied. "They aren't going to buy any mutual funds from me."

Don's response hit me like a ton of bricks. He was right—I absolutely was wasting my prime time at the coffee shop and it wasn't helping my career. From that day on, I decided I would no longer spend time on unproductive coffee breaks. From people like Don Slater, I learned the importance of focusing with intensity on what you need to do to achieve your aims.

If you consider some of the most successful people in the world today, from athletes to CEOs and world leaders, their focus has been critical to their success. Achieving focus means directing your energy to a defined purpose.

If you've ever tried to light a fire by directing sunlight through a magnifying glass, you know you need a defined target and directed energy—in other words, the sun. If you are patient, committed and focused on your target, eventually you'll start a fire.

In your life, when you direct your focus, energies and actions at a defined target, you stand a far better chance of realizing success.

TUNE OUT DISTRACTIONS

The key to becoming better focused is to learn how to tune out distractions. It's not easy in this BlackBerry-driven and multi-channel-TV universe. Many people have so much going on in their lives at once that they feel scattered and unable to concentrate. They strive for results but are unable to produce them. It can be overwhelming.

Comedian George Carlin summed up well why we have trouble achieving focus:

The paradox of our time in history is that we have taller buildings but shorter tempers, wider freeways, but narrower viewpoints. We spend more, but have less; we buy more, but enjoy less. We have bigger houses and smaller families, more conveniences, but less time. We have more degrees but less sense, more knowledge, but less judgment, more experts, yet more problems, more medicine, but less wellness. We drink too much, smoke too much, spend too recklessly, laugh too little, drive too fast, get too angry, stay up too late, get up too tired, read too little, watch TV too much, and pray too seldom. We have multiplied our possessions, but reduced our values. We talk too much, love too seldom, and hate too often. We've learned how to make a living, but not a life. We've added years to life, not life to years.

The ability to multitask is considered a must to achieve success, but what some people consider multitasking is in reality giving in to distractions. In his book *The Myth of Multitasking*, author Dave Crenshaw argues that "doing it all" gets nothing done. For Crenshaw, multitasking is inefficient because it wastes time and money, and erodes relationships. He argues it is much more efficient to do one thing at a time, with focus.

In fact, the most successful multitaskers have incredible focus. Take an emergency room doctor, for example. He or she must have the ability to multitask, but also needs to focus intently when making life-or-death diagnoses. Journalists rely on the ability to multitask while meeting tight deadlines. Award-winning journalist Diane Sawyer once said a lesson she learned over the years is that "there is no substitute for paying attention."

Florence Chadwick was a champion swimmer who wanted to set the record for swimming the English Channel. Chadwick felt as prepared as she would ever be on the day she stepped into the cold waves of the Channel, her body greased to provide insulation against the biting cold. The Atlantic was unusually rough that day, but Chadwick wasn't bothered—she had trained for it. Besides, she had the support of her trainers who rowed alongside her, feeding her soup and talking to her. The only thing Chadwick hadn't counted on was the heavy fog. It soon engulfed her. She began to lose her bearings. As the fog grew denser, she felt less able to cope with the cold and the high waves. Her limbs began to cramp. Finally, she was forced to quit, and learned later she was just one mile from her destination. When the media later asked her why she had given up when the shore was so close, she said, "I lost sight of my goal. I'm not sure I ever had it firmly in mind."

The story of Florence Chadwick points to the essential need to remain focused on what you want to achieve, and to keep your goal in mind, even when life tosses in unexpected surprises. Her story isn't one of failure, because she learned from that experience. She went on to become the first woman to swim twenty-three miles across the English Channel in both directions.

By learning to focus, you can weed out the distractions that prevent you from achieving your dreams.

FOCUS ON YOUR STRENGTHS

Imagine holding a beautiful vase of indigo-coloured water. You set it out on your patio and forget about it overnight. During the night, it rains. When you remember the vase in the morning, you find it overflowing; the water is no longer indigo. It is a weak blue, almost clear. Our lives are like that. Many of us have remarkable strengths that we water down by adding too many elements. Soon, we feel we've lost the ability to do anything well.

Your focus is your emotional currency. Spend it on the thoughts and feelings that enrich your life instead of on those that drain your energy and reinforce a negative mindset. What you focus on expands in direct proportion to the amount of time you spend on it.

Most successful people possess a laser-beam ability to focus on the task at hand. This ranges from the professional hockey team that must block out doubting press before the Stanley Cup final, to a prime minister or president who must make sound decisions despite the constant criticism that is part of the political system.

Former world heavyweight champion George Foreman was able to deflect anything that took away from the positive energy he needed to win. "That's my gift," Foreman said. "I let that negativity roll off me like water off a duck's back. If it's not positive, I didn't hear it. If you can overcome that, fights are easy."

What separates many successful people from the rest of the pack is they can focus on their strengths and not on criticism or failure.

ACT ON YOUR PRIORITIES

Too often, we wait until our lives are in crisis before we begin to make adjustments to our priorities. Wherever you are in life, and whatever situation you're in, it's important to make changes, starting today, that will lead you to a more streamlined way of living. It will also help you better cope with the tough stuff that comes up in your life. Here are a few steps to get you started:

Step 1: Reflect on your priorities. What types of things consistently draw your attention? Where do you spend the majority of your time? What issues tend to make you drop everything and cancel plans in order to address them? Try to imagine yourself in a variety of situations. What might pull you away from an important project at work or from time with your family?

Step 2: Consider your priorities in light of your values. Do these priorities reflect what you truly believe to be most important to you? Keep your list of priorities handy so you can refer to it again as you define goals and plans for each of your values.

Step 3: Remain flexible enough to adjust your course occasionally when life warrants it, but avoid the "candle in the wind" approach, where you allow circumstances to blow you in different directions. If you continually allow this to happen, you'll soon find your light dimmed or extinguished.

One way to focus your life so that it's in line with your values is to decide what you want to accomplish every day and write it down in a daily activity diary. Set your intentions and make them clear. My list is known as my MITs, or Most Important Things. It is a focal point for my energies, and it contains things I feel are most important in my life, including business, personal and family priorities. Each night before I go to bed I write down my MITs for the following day. I also make sure they are aligned with my values.

Some of you might read this and say, "Sure Peter, that's easier said than done." Some of you may have young children to get ready for school, or aging parents to look after, as well as your own business and personal life to take care of. My response is that if you *really* want more focus and happiness in life, it is important to find five minutes each day to create your list of priorities. It doesn't matter who you are, how much money you have, where you live or what you do, the success of your day depends on how closely you follow your list of priorities.

By defining your values and checking in with them on a regular basis, you'll begin to notice patterns. It may be that a certain person in your life is always asking you to adjust your priorities. It may also be that you are cramming too much activity into your life and constantly running up against impossible deadlines that force you to compromise. You will learn from these patterns and be able to prioritize what's important to you, spending less time on the negative and more time on the positive parts of your life.

CHAPTER 6

LEARN TO RUMBA

O nce you've identified the values that will be your navigational tools, and learned to apply the power of focus, it's time to define your destination—in other words, set goals.

Author Napoleon Hill wrote, "A goal is a dream with a deadline." If you look deep enough you'll find your dreams almost always arise from what you truly value in life. Goal setting is the alchemy that turns those dreams into reality.

I think the reason many people don't achieve success is because they don't practise regular goal setting. Goals are absolutely essential to accomplish anything worthwhile, not just in a business or a career but in your personal life as well. Goal setting gives you direction. Without goals, you are like a ship without a rudder, bounced around by good winds and bad, never knowing where you're going to wind up. I set goals for everything—every single solitary aspect of my life. My personal definition of success is the achievement of any goal a person sets in his or her life, from flying a kite to becoming a CEO. I strongly recommend that anyone who wants to be great prioritize their life and activities by establishing long-term and short-term goals and revisiting them regularly.

The ability to set and achieve goals—be they working through the everyday "to-do" list or hitting a major objective—will define your life and be the difference between success and disappointment. Once you set these goals, and align them with your values, you can get what you want out of life, instead of having to experience want from life.

To help you clearly articulate your goals, I want to share with you my method of writing goals, motivating myself and focusing on my energies. It is called RUMBA—yes, like the dance. To really RUMBA, your goals must be realistic, understandable, meaningful and measurable, believable and agreed. When you set goals based on these principles and put them into action, you actively determine the way you will live your life rather than just allowing life to happen to you.

Realistic: Your goals must have some basis in reality. Make sure you have a clear idea of what you want to achieve and what is required to succeed. Do you have the prerequisites, or do you have to prepare? If so, you may decide to readjust your goals to include the various steps you need to achieve before targeting your big goal. Also, it's important to take into account how much time and energy you can realistically devote to your goals.

Understandable: Describe your goals using specific language so you are very clear about what you want to achieve. For instance, saying that you will save money for a trip isn't as clear as saying you will set aside $400 a month for the next twelve months to reach your goal.

Meaningful and measurable: Your goals should be important to you. They should not be things others think you should do. Instead, they are what you choose to do as part of your commitment to a better life. When you set your goals, be as specific as possible. Whenever you can, create timelines, benchmarks for achievement and deadlines. If you plan to lose twenty pounds, break the weight loss into weekly or monthly goals. After all, what gets measured gets done.

Believable: If you don't believe you can reach your goal, you won't be motivated to attain it. A prime example is the smoker who, out of guilt, promises to quit but doesn't really believe he can do it. Without the inner belief that he can triumph over addiction, is it any wonder he is sneaking cigarettes within a matter of weeks of quitting?

Agreed: If you set personal goals and don't share them with anyone, you often lose the benefits, encouragement and fun of involving stakeholders in your success. A surefire way to help yourself stay focused on your preset goals is to share those goals with people who are important in your life—your spouse, your employer, your friends, your mentors and anyone else who will be affected either by your drive to accomplish your goals or by your success.

Not only do successful people set goals and discipline themselves to achieve them, but they also document their goals in lists, letters, pictures or whatever medium suits them best. They know that if they don't have a plan and work toward achieving it, they are in danger of soon becoming part of someone else's plan.

My longtime friend Ken Marlin is a founder of many successful companies, including First Investors Corporation and Marlin Travel. Ken spends his "retirement years" mentoring people to achieve financial freedom. He is a great believer in writing things down and setting goals for the day.

"When you do this," says Ken, "you are in control of your time, and it is not in control of you." In fact, Ken took this goal-setting practice beyond the personal; he applied this philosophy to motivate his team at First Investors. Every day, Ken held a forty-five-minute morning meeting that every team member was required to attend. When people achieved their goals, they received a round of applause. No recriminations were delivered during those meetings to those who didn't reach their goals. They simply didn't get the positive reinforcement of applause.

START SMALL, BUT START NOW

Maybe you see goal setting as too structured, impeding your ability to "go with the flow." I believe that when you fail to set goals, you fail to use an important tool in determining your future. If you find yourself unable to set big, lofty goals, start small. Late night talk-show host David Letterman's goal is ambitious and humble. "I'm just trying to make a smudge on the collective unconscious," he says. And he does.

As the nineteenth-century Russian writer Ivan Turgenev told us, "If we wait for the moment when everything, absolutely everything, is ready we shall never begin." The same can be said for setting goals. Don't wait for the New Year, your next paycheque or even when the day is over. Start now. If you haven't set goals before, start with just your goals for the next twelve months. This will help you focus on what you can achieve in the near future. Later, you can explore long-term goals, those you hope to achieve in three to five years.

Also, keep your goals specific. If they are too abstract you will lower your chances of achieving them. As Eleanor Roosevelt said, "Happiness is not a goal; it is a by-product." What she wisely knew was that abstract goals such as happiness, peace of mind and success can only be achieved by setting and accomplishing concrete goals.

Scott Adams is a prime example of someone who set realistic, achievable goals that ultimately led to bigger and bigger goals. At thirty, Scott was a middle manager sitting in a cubicle and dreaming of becoming a cartoonist. Scott began to realize he would never fulfill his dream unless he set goals for himself. He decided he would start by trying to get published in just one place before his life was over. He created a package of cartoon strips about a middle manager lost in the corporate maze. A decade later, everyone knows the cartoon strip *Dilbert*. It's published in a thousand newspapers and in more than thirty countries. It all began with Scott Adams' goal to publish just one cartoon strip before he died.

Like Scott Adams, I set achievable goals. I had been a runner all my life until my back started aching so badly I could no longer do it. Thirty years of running had done its damage. All you runners out there know what kind of a sentence this is after a lifetime of running. As I started to gain weight, I realized I had to do something. I turned to the exercise bike with horror. All of my life, I had wondered how anyone could ride those bikes while it was so great outside—the air, the weather, the freedom! There was no way I wanted to ride that exercise bike inside a gym or at home, but it was obvious I had a decision to make. I knew that if I kept on doing what I was doing, which was nothing, I wasn't going to like what I saw in the mirror. I decided that instead of setting a goal to ride the bike for twenty minutes at a time, I would only ride it for five minutes a day. This was something I could do whether I liked being on the bike or not. Well, very quickly my five minutes expanded to ten, and then twenty and then thirty minutes. Now I can't imagine not riding my bike for thirty minutes a day.

By starting out with a smaller goal, I didn't set myself up for failure but for victory. I now do this with any project I find difficult to get excited about. The only thing you have to do is show up dressed and committed—your natural momentum will take over. Trust yourself and get out of your own way. START NOW, no matter how daunting the task may seem.

ALIGN GOALS WITH VALUES

While I firmly believe the ability to achieve predetermined goals is a major success factor, I know that unless those goals are aligned with your values, you may end up at a destination you don't like. As you set goals, remember to check back frequently with your values. Do your goals and values align? If they don't, you may need to change your goals or go back and better define your values.

For example, suppose your partner schedules an important business dinner on the night you are having dinner with your parents. You feel guilty, so you cancel your family dinner for the business one. Or, maybe your employer demands that you work late every second night to finish projects, so you miss spending time with your children. These are examples of the way we put our own values and goals aside to meet the needs of others, often out of guilt, fear or a need to please.

That's exactly what happened to my friend, entrepreneur John Papaloukas. A few years ago, John attended a conference in Boston at the Massachusetts Institute of Technology. It was a big and important event, but John and a group of others complained to the organizers about it happening over the Father's Day weekend. They told them it didn't make sense, since many of the participants were parents, and recommended the date be changed the following year. A year later, when John received his conference agenda, he noted that it was once again scheduled for Father's Day. "I said, 'No offense, but I'm not attending. A group of us asked you not to have it on Father's Day. I've got two children at home, my wife was disappointed last year, so no, I won't be coming this year. I want to spend Father's Day with my family.'"

By setting your priorities, you'll begin to create order in your life and give yourself permission to make choices that align with your values. Sure, you still occasionally may have to deal with other people's needs and demands, but now you have the tools to make conscious choices about the way you spend your time, from a position of strength and awareness, not from uncertainty and guilt.

CHAPTER 7

THREE LUXURIES YOU CAN'T AFFORD

When I was a young boy I liked to draw. One day, in Grade 2 art class, my teacher, Miss Belmont, asked everyone to draw a picture of a cow. I drew the best picture I could. I was quite happy with my cow, and Miss Belmont approached my desk and held up the picture for the class to see. They all laughed at my rendition of a cow. I lost any desire to draw again.

Much later in life, when I was in my forties, I went to an art gallery and saw one of Pablo Picasso's depictions of cows. I thought, "My cow was much better than his!"—yet I had let my classmates' laughter convince me I had done a poor job. Surprisingly, I one day read a quotation from Picasso that said, "Every child is an artist. The problem is how to remain an artist once he grows up."

By reflecting on this story from my youth, I learned that there are three factors that inhibit us from reaching our goals and achieving our potential. These factors are fear, uncertainty and doubt, or what I call FUD. When we give into FUD, we set ourselves up for failure.

IS FEAR HOLDING YOU BACK?

Knowing what we now know about goal setting, why would anyone choose not to exercise that power? Some people avoid setting goals because they fear failure. Often, that fear becomes a self-fulfilling prophecy. Still others fear the changes that may result from actually achieving their goals. For these people, "dreams that do come true can be as unsettling as those that don't," says comedian Brett Butler in her bestseller, *Knee Deep in Paradise*.

An example of this is Maya, who for years has dreamed of returning to university to finish her Master of Business degree. But Maya has refused to turn her daydream into an actual goal. "Then I would have to do it and I don't know how I'd feel about being a fifty-year-old with all the twenty-somethings," she says. "Also, my family would have to fend for themselves more and my husband wouldn't be too happy with that."

Maya's "but" list goes on and on. What she really fears is success, because it will change her life and take her out of her comfort zone. In Maya's mind, giving up on her dream is a small price to pay for maintaining family harmony. The question is: can a family be truly harmonious if one member has to pay such a high price? There are many "what ifs" that might happen when we set goals, but that's all they are. Everything we do in life is cause and effect, after all.

I believe if my intentions are good and my goals are aligned with my values, I will accomplish my goals. I can't let fear of what might happen stop me.

"In order to succeed," says comedian and actor Bill Cosby, "your desire for success should be greater than your fear of failure."

It's important to put fear into perspective, which is exactly what world champion cyclist Lance Armstrong did when he was diagnosed with cancer. In his book *It's Not About the Bike*, he wrote, "I thought I knew what fear was, until I heard the words, 'you have cancer.' Real fear came with an unmistakable sensation; it was as though all my blood started flowing in the wrong direction. My previous fears, fear of not being liked, fear of being laughed at, fear of losing my money, suddenly seemed like small cowardice. Everything now stacked up differently: the anxieties of life—a flat tire, losing my career, a traffic jam—were reprioritized into need versus want, real problems as opposed to minor scares. A bumpy plane ride was just a bumpy plane ride, it wasn't cancer."

Hopefully, you will never have to deal with a serious illness to put your own fears into perspective.

Here's an exercise: Take a measuring tape out of your toolbox. Extend it to eighty inches, which is the same number as the average life span of a typical Canadian. Now count off how old you are today, using one inch for every year. Look at the time you have left. What are you going to do about it and when are you going to let go of the fears that prevent you from living life to the fullest? If you're lucky, you will have a nice, long life ahead of you, but be aware that the measuring tape can retract suddenly, as measuring tapes sometimes do. Don't let fear hold you back from the life you want.

WHERE DOES YOUR UNCERTAINTY COME FROM?

If your uncertainty isn't just about achieving a goal, but goes deeper into the core of who you are, you need to raise your self-esteem. Psychologist William James believed that to improve your chances of attaining your goals, you could do one of two things: lower your goals to meet your low self-esteem or raise your self-esteem to meet your goals.

I've never been one to lower my goals. As an example, even though I never set out with the lofty dream of becoming a multi-millionaire, I always set myself a goal of reaching higher than wherever I was. To do that, I had to believe in my ability to achieve the next stage of success. I never for a minute considered lowering my goals. I chose growth and believed that I was equal to my aspirations.

I encourage you to think of the things you value about yourself. Often, you'll find what you value most about yourself complements the values you chose as the guiding principles of your life. Don't just focus on your accomplishments to date; look deeper and you may uncover assets that are sleeping within you and only need to be awakened. I've received letters from many people saying they discovered parts of themselves they had ignored or felt uncertain about. An example of this is Sean, who came to one of my LifePilot workshops as an overstressed CEO with dangerously high blood pressure and anxiety so heavy that he often fantasized about walking away from everything. When I asked the audience to list their values, Sean began a journey that helped him remember why he had started his business in the first place. It wasn't to sit in boardrooms all day. It wasn't to become what his investors, his staff and his clients thought he should be. It was to make a difference in the world and help people. Years of working in an environment that constantly grated against his core values had worn down his belief in himself to the point where he felt powerless to make a difference.

Sean decided to make some changes. He began taking solitary walks for up to two hours a day. His weight dropped. He started sleeping better. His relationships with his friends and family began to heal and he began to feel more certain about his future. He became inspired again—not for his business but for his life. He discovered the person he really is beneath the CEO title and constant demands of meeting payroll.

Not only did he dig deep into his own meaning, but Sean also opened his mind to the people who loved him and were only too happy to tell him about his positive attributes. He began moving away from relationships that shattered his belief in himself, and set boundaries around the kinds of behaviour he would accept from others. He also literally moved to a new city where he could be away from the stress that surrounded his business life, and allowed himself to refocus on what is important to him, in particular his health, happiness and building a stronger relationship with his long-time girlfriend.

"Looking at my values and goals was a wake-up call to me," Sean says. "I was on a collision course. Through goal setting, I've begun to articulate what I do want, not just what I don't want. It feels good."

Today, Sean is healthy and happy in a wonderful relationship. He has determined where his uncertainty in himself came from, enabling him to build the mental and physical strength to fight those business battles that caused him so much stress to begin with.

DO YOU DOUBT YOUR ABILITY?

When you doubt your ability to achieve a goal, you dramatically lower the odds of reaching it. When in doubt, try using my favourite motto: "It's easy; it's a piece of cake." Not a day goes by that I don't remind myself of this sentence. For some reason, it helps me accomplish things I cannot normally imagine myself doing.

I remember a time when I was the auctioneer raising funds at an event put together by Canadian-born record producer David Foster. I told David we could raise $100,000 and needed twenty minutes to do it. David thought it would be easier to raise funds by getting extra sponsors or selling more tickets. He eventually agreed to the auction and the timing, but wanted a guarantee that the full sum of money would be raised. "Absolutely," I said, although inside I wasn't completely sure if I could pull it off.

The auction went ahead. When it was time for the last item, we had raised only $35,000, or about one-third of what I promised. The last of the items was some tickets for the final Barbra Streisand concert. We had one bidder. I tried not to worry. Instead, I got one of my friends to join in and create a bidding war. I watched him slowly turn blue as the bidding crept up to $30,000, then $40,000, then $50,000. The winning bid was $65,000. My friend didn't win the tickets, which to him was a relief. I never doubted we could raise those funds, although I admit I was also relieved when the auction ended and we had reached our goal.

If after challenging your fears you still feel tentative, contemplating all the things that could go amiss as you try to reach your goals, ask yourself if worrying about "what ifs" is a good reason to do nothing. When I think about the energy we waste on worrying, I'm reminded of a story involving the famous Italian conductor Arturo Toscanini. Once, shortly before a prestigious concert in front of a standing-room-only audience, a member of Toscanini's orchestra approached the conductor in a state of heavy anxiety. "Maestro," the musician said, "my instrument is not working properly. I can't reach the note of E-flat. I'm beside myself with worry and the concert will begin in just a few minutes." Toscanini smiled and put his arm around the man's shoulders. "My friend," the maestro said, "do not worry about it. The note E-flat does not appear anywhere in the music you will be playing this evening."

Brian Tracy, author of *Create Your Own Future*, writes, "Your greatest limits are not external. They are internal, within your thinking. These are contained in your personal self-limiting beliefs. These are beliefs that act as brakes on your potential. These are beliefs that cause you to sell yourself short, and to settle for far less than you are truly capable of."

Now that you are able to recognize the FUD that has been holding you back, let's talk more about building the better, more confident you.

CHAPTER 8

CREATE YOUR PERSONAL BRAND

I'm a country music fan, so when I had the opportunity to see Reba McIntyre in concert I was ecstatic. From the moment she stepped on stage, it was electrifying. Her voice was fierce and powerful, clear and passionate, a voice that could belong to no one else but Reba.

When Reba takes the stage, it feels like she's making eye contact with you and only you. She connects with her audience in a very personal, intimate way. I left the concert with one powerful thought: "Reba was into her song."

When you start living in tune with your values, you'll be into your song, too. You will develop what I call a personal brand—the way you showcase your positive influence and convey the essence of who you are.

Your brand is a combination of the way you look, communicate and act. Think of President Barack Obama, businessmen Richard Branson and Donald Trump, musicians Madonna and Celine Dion, and celebrity interviewer Oprah Winfrey. Each name brings to mind a different image and sensation based on a combination of appearance and accomplishment. Personal branding is important, whether you're in the public eye or not. Developing a compelling personal brand helps people see you more clearly. When they do, they will feel drawn to you and be willing to be engaged.

SHOW THE WORLD WHO YOU REALLY ARE

We have all heard the saying "You will never get a second chance to make a first impression." Experts say people usually form a first impression within the first thirty seconds of meeting someone new and if you want to change that impression it can take an extra twenty more experiences to do it.

When you meet people for the first time, all of their gut instincts come into play. They either consciously or unconsciously come up with an impression of you based on the way you look, dress, talk, smile or frown, and behave. Unknowingly, they are really thinking about your brand—your advertisement—and forming an enduring impression. Personal branding is a way to showcase your positive influence and convey the essence of who you are.

Even if you don't crave the limelight, you need to be aware of branding. Developing a compelling brand helps people see you more clearly. When they do, they begin to feel more drawn to you and what you have to offer. The most effective branding helps your family, friends, co-workers, peers and employers understand the essence of who you are. You begin to walk your talk and, as a result, you'll find you have to spend less time explaining who you are or justifying your ideas.

In his book *The Brand Called You*, author Peter Montoya says, "Personal branding lets you control how other people perceive you . . . You're telling them what you stand for—but in a way that's so organic and unobtrusive that they think they've developed that perception all by themselves."

THE BASICS OF PERSONAL BRANDING

William Arruda, founder of the branding company Reach, says all strong brands have three main things in common; clarity, consistency and constancy. They are what he calls "The Three Cs of Personal Branding."

Clarity: "Strong brands are clear about who they are and who they are not," says Arruda. "They understand their unique promise of value." In this example, Arruda points to flamboyant entrepreneur Richard Branson, the man behind the Virgin Group of Companies, which has subsidiaries that reach into thirty countries and products that range from music stores to cell phones and even an airline. However, Branson is not your typical CEO. He is known as a risk taker and a bit of a corporate stuntman. He is known for having dressed in a wedding gown when he launched his bridal shop named Virgin Brides, and wearing nothing at all when he launched his book, *Losing My Virginity*. His first big risky venture was signing the band the Sex Pistols when nobody else would. While I'm not suggesting you should do what Branson does to promote your brand, you get the point. Branson's brand is big and he builds it every day.

Consistency: To be consistent with your personal brand, you don't have to do the same thing every day. Consistency means sticking with a common theme. It's about developing a trademark and allowing it to grow and change with the times. Al Pacino is a good example of an actor who has a consistent brand. From his roles in *The Godfather* series to *Scarface*, *City Hall* and other films, we expect Pacino to play strong characters and deliver solid performances. Singer Madonna is another great example of a consistent brand that Arruda uses. While she reinvents herself with each CD she produces, Arruda reminds us that Madonna "changes with incredible consistency . . . each time starting a trend. Her ability to change consistently throughout her career separates her from other entertainers, thereby strengthening her brand."

Constancy: Arruda says it's not enough to be clear and consistent. You also have to be visible to your audience. "Strong brands are constant," he says, using Oprah Winfrey as an example. He points to her weekly television shows, her book club, her magazine and other appearances. "Oprah is the human brand of show biz. She cares for people and is willing to share of herself to help people advance. This clarity about what makes her unique is consistent among all of her endeavours. And it is constantly visible to her target audience through her numerous ways of interacting with the public."

We all have a brand or image we project, whether we're famous or not. Remember, none of these people was famous throughout his or her entire life. They only became so through a combination of talent and developing their personal brand. When you start living in tune with your values, you will naturally feel more confident and ready to show the world the "real you."

TAKE CHARGE OF YOUR BRAND

You are in charge of your brand, from the clothes you wear to the friends you keep, to the career and clients you choose. Everything you do radiates who you are. On the popular TV show *What Not to Wear*, two fashion and image experts work with people in need of makeovers and personal branding.

While the audience can see that these people are not show-casing their best attributes, the people themselves often don't. They usually wind up on the show on the recommendation of friends or family. At first, many of the participants worry that the makeover process will hide who they really are. But once they've gone through the makeover—which simply includes some new, more flattering clothes and a new hairstyle—they generally end up feeling that the person buried inside finally is being allowed to shine. On this show, artists don't come out looking like executives. They look like successful artists. Bike couriers don't look like ballerinas. They just make a better first impression and convey more of the essence of who they really are.

CHECK IN WITH YOUR BRAND

I like to think of my brand as a good leader who is enthusiastic, trustworthy, healthy and hardworking. Not only is that who I am, but it's also the brand I've worked hard to maintain throughout the years. It comes from my values. Everything I do and believe in supports these principles. My mother used to tell me to imagine everything I did would one day be written across the sky for everyone to read. I felt I had better do good things if I wanted to see good things up there.

My friend Praveen Varshney, director of investment company Varshney Capital Corp., based in Vancouver, believes personal brand equity is critical in today's society.

"The essence of a brand is the mental imprint we plant on the minds of our market and people around us (even people we don't know)."

Praveen's personal brand starts with his integrity, and to him there are two types of it: internal and external. Internal integrity is being true to yourself, your values, beliefs, principles and what he calls "the big test—which is how you act when nobody is watching." External integrity, Praveen says, means "saying what you mean and doing what you say." Better still is UPOD, an acronym Praveen came up (and has trademarked), which stands for underpromise and overdeliver so you exceed all your promises. "Most people do the opposite," says Praveen. "They *OPUD*—overpromise and underdeliver. They say the things they think other people want to hear and set them and others up for disappointment." Adds Praveen, "I don't know a single person that doesn't like a pleasant surprise! By successfully and consistently following UPOD, you become the 'go-to guy' that everyone wants on their team, or to do business with. The secret to successfully UPOD'ing is to set and manage expectations well, your own or someone else's."

Praveen has enjoyed a successful career but none of the external trappings of success are as vital to him as maintaining his personal integrity. This integrity is about acting in alignment with his values and belief systems and having a strong moral compass. "Integrity, a standard of personal morality and ethics, is not relative to the situation you happen to find yourself in and doesn't sell out to expediency," he says. Praveen checks in with his personal integrity when making decisions by asking himself what kind of role model he wants to be for his kids.

CREATE YOUR PERSONAL MISSION STATEMENT

To begin bringing out your strengths and developing your brand, ask yourself these questions: What makes me different from everyone else? What are my most admirable character traits? What do most people identify me with? In what ways do I demonstrate my values to others? What parts of myself am I totally comfortable with, and what parts make me feel awkward, as though I am wearing a pair of ill-fitting shoes? Do I dress for success and confidence, or do I just "throw something on?" Do my clothes reflect my personality in the best possible way?

To help you focus on what you want to project to the world through your personal brand, I recommend creating your own mission statement. This statement should say who you are and what you want to communicate most to the people you meet. To assist you, here's one example of a mission statement written by a LifePilot participant:

I will live a life of authenticity, originality, adventure and discovery. People will identify me with a warm smile, lack of pretension, strong handshake and high fitness level. I will project the courage to go farther than others to make discoveries. I will travel throughout the world in my quest. I will be energized, fulfilled, and inspired.

A longtime friend of mine, Jamesie Bower, found a great deal of value in writing her mission statement—with some unexpected surprises.

In 2002, Jamesie was driving home from work, thinking about the mission statement she had been asked to write as part of her LifePilot workshop. "I wanted to write something that highlighted the positive energy I have been blessed with, so I was very excited," she recalls. As a busy professional, Jamesie typically followed a solid routine to keep her life on track. But that evening, instead of getting changed out of her work clothes and taking off her jewellery before launching into her chores, she plunged right into cleaning her kitchen so she could get straight to her LifePilot homework. The next morning, as she was getting ready for an early appointment, Jamesie looked on the dresser where she usually kept her rings. They weren't there. They weren't anywhere in the house.

At that point she realized what she must have done. Tossing out the garbage the night before, she had somehow thrown away her rings. "I was absolutely frantic," she recalls, "because those rings had a great deal of meaning to me. That feeling stayed with me on my drive to work, but then, as I was driving across the Lions Gate Bridge in Vancouver,

I suddenly had an epiphany. I thought to myself, 'J.B., there are thousands of women with more diamonds than you will ever possess. Get over it!'"

Jamesie realized that her diamonds did not define her. What glittered most about Jamesie—and still does—is that remarkable, sparkling energy that no diamonds could ever possess. That energy was the focus of the mission statement she had written. Oddly enough, when Jamesie went to lunch that day with friends, they inadvertently joined a table of people whose business was diamond exploration. She told them her story and they joked about "exploring" the garbage for Jamesie's diamonds. She never did find the diamonds, but she found something far more valuable: her worth beyond jewels.

Creating your personal mission statement—one that embodies your values, ambitions and long-term goals—will provide a foundation on which to build your future aspirations and an internal guide for everyday living.

Now that we have covered the bases of how to identify your values and focus your life on attaining your goals, let's talk about how to visualize and make your dreams a reality.

FOUNDATION 3:

VISUALIZATION

CHAPTER 9

SEE IT, HAVE IT

Men live to impress the women they love. Before we married, Rita and I had been seeing each other for about a year when she invited me to go skiing in Whistler, British Columbia, a top-rated ski area. I'm fairly athletic, but I hadn't skied since I left home at age fifteen. Naturally, I said yes. I didn't tell Rita I barely knew how to ski. But I came up with a plan. I bought videos by French Olympic ski champion Jean-Claude Killy so that I could watch them and learn from the master. My goal was to watch the videos right away, but days and weeks passed and I became too busy to sit down and do it. Finally, it was the day of the ski trip and I still hadn't seen the tapes. I decided not to panic. At the time I had a car and driver and decided I would watch them on the three-hour drive to Whistler. I sat in the back of the car and watched those tapes over and over again until we arrived at the resort.

A few hours later, Rita and I stepped into our skis, hopped on the chairlift, and headed up the mountain. Fortunately, I managed to make it out of the chair without toppling over. Just as I was quietly congratulating myself, Rita tipped her skis to the left and veered straight down one of the steepest slopes I had ever seen. I gulped and, taking a deep breath, off I went. My form might not have been as good as Jean-Claude Killy's or Rita's, but I did make it down that slope pretty well—and in one piece. I know it was 100 per cent from watching those videos. To me, that's the power of visualization, the third foundation of an extraordinary life.

Old sayings such as "What you can see, you can achieve" don't form in a vacuum. Visualization—the art of using mental imagery to produce positive changes in your life—works. For years top achievers, from the golf course to the boardroom, have been using this technique to reach peak performance. It's as critical a part of their careers, and ultimate success, as the gruelling hours of practice and physical preparation.

Your imagination is extremely powerful. Once you create a picture in your mind of the way you'd like things to be or what you'd like to have, your mind begins to move toward making it real.

WHAT YOU SEE IS WHAT YOU GET

Many successful people, from business people to athletes and celebrities, have used visualization to achieve their goals. As far as they're concerned, it's not a matter of "if" they will achieve their dreams—it's a matter of "when." This focus and passion for achieving a goal creates energy to which others respond.

Research has shown that both physical and psychological results can be improved with visualization. Professional athletes are some of the strongest proponents of creative visualization, and many use it as part of their training. Michael Phelps, the U.S. swimmer who won an amazing eight gold medals at the 2008 Olympics, credits visualization as one of the keys to his success. In his book *Beneath the Surface*, Phelps says, "When I'm about to fall asleep, I visualize to the point that I know exactly what I want to do: dive, glide, stroke, flip, reach the wall, hit the split time to the hundredth, then swim back again for as many times as I need to finish the race."

At age twelve, now-famous golfer Tiger Woods visualized himself winning the Masters Tournament. He pictured every step from the last putt: the ball rolling toward the cup, the crowd cheering and himself receiving the trophy while wearing the green victory jacket. Then he pushed ahead with the necessary training to achieve that goal, which he did a decade later by a record margin of twelve strokes, becoming the youngest Masters winner in history. He went on to set a total of twenty Masters records and tied six others. Woods is known for his pre-game visualization. His caddie, Steve Williams, told *Golf Digest* in 2008 after a game that, "instead of spending hours on the practice field, he just tried to picture how he wanted to swing the club."

Walt Disney was a believer in creative visualization. One day as he sat on a bench at an amusement park, watching his daughters play, he noticed how dirty the park was. He also noticed that the kids' parents were all anxious to leave, even though the kids were having fun. He began to visualize a better amusement park, a clean, safe place that could be enjoyed by children and parents alike. That idea became Disneyland. Before building the world's largest theme park, Disney travelled throughout the United States. He visited Thomas Edison's workshop, the Wright Brothers' bicycle shop, and the home of dictionary magnate Noah Webster. As he travelled and reflected, Disney began to build Disneyland in his mind. The park then became a reality that has attracted families from around the world. Both kids and parents enjoy it, just as Disney visualized they would. Walt Disney died of throat cancer in 1966, but not before purchasing 28,000 acres of swampland in Florida—or what would become his second theme park, Disney World. He never saw Disney World created. But he didn't have to. He had pictured it in his mind enough times.

FOCUS ON A POSITIVE PICTURE

Have you ever pictured yourself climbing a podium to accept an award? Do you picture yourself smiling and waving to an applauding crowd, or do you see yourself tripping on the way up the stairs or dropping the statue? Successful people focus on a positive picture of the future, whereas unsuccessful people lose positive perspective by focusing on problems and fears. People who walk around with a cloud over their head, complaining that they are unlucky, unloved or unattractive are making those things a reality because that is how they see themselves. On the other hand, people who believe they are fortunate, attractive and have great relationships are making that their reality, simply because that is how they see themselves.

If you think of the good things you want to happen in your life, you are creating positive energy, and chances are the good things will come about. That is because what we visualize reinforces the way we approach our lives. The world we believe we live in is, in fact, the world we live in. To discover a successful future, we need to visualize it. For some of us, this might mean we need to change our vision of our lives and ask, "Which movie do I want to star in?" Sometimes the results are truly amazing.

My friend Alfredo J. Molina is the owner of Molina Fine Jewelers in Phoenix, Arizona. Over the years, Alfredo has built up a remarkable business with a tradition of excellence that dates back to the Italian Renaissance but, like so many of us, he began with nothing. He remembers arriving in the United States as a young boy, a refugee from Cuba. His family's first American home was in Chicago, where the Catholic Diocese took them in and put them up at the Wilson Hotel, which was condemned and torn down just months later. Somewhere along the way, Alfredo developed the belief that the unconscious mind is a powerful thing. He combined hard work with visualization to realize his success. He visualized his Phoenix store out of what had previously been a parking lot. Today, Molina Fine Jewelers is housed in one of the city's most beautiful buildings. What's more, the home he ended up living in is the same home he clipped out a picture of years ago to help him visualize his goal.

Visualization can also help you get through some very trying times. One of the most fascinating stories of the power of visualization is that of Air Force Colonel George Hall, who was captured by the North Vietnamese in 1965 and imprisoned in a dark box for seven years. For each day of those seven long years, Hall played a full game of golf in his mind. Every detail of his imaginary game was real to him, from the Titleist balls to the blue tees that he placed in the grass still wet from the morning dew. The smell of fresh grass replaced the musty smell of the prison. He mentally played and re-played every golf course he had ever been on. He climbed up the hills, looked out onto the fairways and studied the greens.

In his imagination, he played a good game of golf. One week after his release from the camp, he entered the Greater New Orleans Open. He shot a score of seventy-six.

WHY VISUALIZATION WORKS

The more pragmatic among you may be thinking, "Isn't this the stuff of yogis and mystics? How, in the age of Internet, biotech and reason, can we possibly believe we can create our success by visualizing it?" There are many theories about why creative visualization works. What you ultimately believe is up to you. I only know it has worked in my life and the lives of some of the most successful people I know.

Some people approach visualization on a purely pragmatic level—they believe that when you visualize an outcome, you naturally devote yourself to making it happen. Your focus and hard work result in success.

Others look to neuroscience for answers. Studies have shown that the brain doesn't distinguish between internal and external vision. When we visualize something enough, our body comes to believe the vision is real.

John Assaraf, a former street gang member who broke free from his past to become a multi-millionaire before age thirty, writes about the biological foundations of creative visualization. He believes that we build "cells of recognition" in our memory banks.

"When you continuously focus on an image in your mind," he writes, "every cell in your body is involved in that image . . . it eventually becomes 'fixed' and you automatically attract and move toward that which you desire. The reason athletes do this is because they want to condition their mind in such a way that the body automatically behaves the way they want it to without effort. It is the only way to become 'unconsciously competent.' When you visualize the goal over and over again, your body will eventually automatically do whatever it must to make the image a physical reality."

Still others look to quantum physics for answers. Quantum physics teaches that nothing is fixed, that there are no limitations, that everything is vibrating energy. Einstein's famous formula of $E=mc^2$, published in 1905, explains the relationship between energy and matter, namely that energy and matter are interchangeable. Some scientists have taken that formula further, believing that reality is affected by the consciousness observing it, and that nothing in the universe exists independent of our perception of it. In short, we create our own realities.

Whenever we think of doing something, we typically hold two opposing thoughts in our minds: one is that we can do it; the other is that we cannot. By focusing on what we *can* do, success becomes our reality. That's why it's so important to always choose a positive thought!

MAKING VISUALIZATION WORK FOR YOU

You've heard how other people have visualized their goals and achieved them, but how can you do it? First you have to be clear about what you are visualizing. Is it a great presentation you're about to give the next day, a meeting to ask for a raise, or finishing a marathon? Begin by being clear in your own mind about what you want before you set out to visualize it.

Most experts recommend that, to properly visualize your goal, you should be relaxed. Set aside ten or twenty minutes and sit or lie in a comfortable spot where you won't be distracted.

Then, visualize the setting. If it's a meeting with your boss for a raise, picture yourself in his or her office. If it's a marathon, picture the path. And even though it's called "visualization," don't limit yourself to pictures in your mind. Use all of your senses: taste, touch, sound and smell, as well as sight.

What's more, think of all the details. The more detailed you picture your goal or desire, the easier it is to achieve it. For instance, if you are going to ask for a raise, think of the different reactions your boss may have to the request. Then visualize how you will respond. The less detailed the picture, the more difficult it is for your mind to move toward it. Maybe you ask for a raise and your boss says yes, but then asks you how much you want. If you haven't visualized the conversation in detail, you may be caught off guard and risk asking for less than you deserve!

Also, imagine how you will feel after accomplishing your goal: the pride, triumph, satisfaction and excitement you associate with closing that deal, getting that raise or finishing that marathon. Once you've got the picture in your head, think of it casually throughout the day. Reinforce and affirm it. As you focus on your vision, push any doubts away by making strong, positive statements to yourself. State your goal in positive terms with words such as "I will" and not "I wish."

This exercise will help you "see" when the actual event happens. Next, and most importantly, remember to imagine a positive result to your goal. And finally, believe that what you want will happen. Negative thoughts result in negative energy and will only serve to downplay your goals. Believe in yourself!

CHAPTER 10

BELIEVE YOU ALREADY HAVE WHAT YOU WANT

For visualization to really work, you must make the transition from wanting something—a million dollars, a thinner body, a second home, a dream job—to believing that you already possess it. In other words, if you want something you have to believe you already have it, or that you have what it takes to get it. Your subconscious mind does not recognize the difference between a real event or a strongly visualized one. Experts believe this is key behind the power of positive thinking. Athletes, for example, psych themselves up for victory, not for defeat. If you say, "But what if I lose?" the thought will return again and again. If you want to win, you must see yourself winning and then go for it.

That's what I did when I decided to compete in the New York Marathon at age forty-three. I started training one year before the run, but I felt very discouraged. The day after my first training run, I was exhausted. I wasn't sure I was up to the training and needed some extra motivation. To get me through my training, I sat myself down and told myself that I had entered the Olympics as the oldest person to represent his country for the marathon. About a mile before the end of my run each day, I would visualize that I was close to the finish line and thousands of eyes were on me. All of a sudden I would hear the crowd chant "Thomas, Thomas, Thomas," and I'd speed up, racing the last leg as if I was just starting the race. I was creating the enthusiastic emotion of already having won. I was seeing myself as successful, and believing it. I went on to New York, ran the marathon, and left my running partner behind at the halfway mark.

ACCESS THE POWER OF BELIEF

"Visualization is daydreaming with a purpose," wrote author Bo Bennett in *Year to Success*. Many people will tell you that in order for visualization to work, you must make the transition from wanting something to the belief that you already possess it.

Scientist Nikola Tesla, a pioneer in electrical engineering at the turn of the twentieth century, said, "When I get a new idea, I start at once building it up in my imagination, and make improvements and operate the device in my mind.

When I have gone so far as to embody everything in my invention, every possible improvement I can think of, and when I see no fault anywhere, I put into concrete form the final product of my brain." For Tesla, the idea came into existence in his mind long before he built anything.

For me, focusing on photographs helps me solidify images in my mind of what I want to achieve. I do this to prepare for public speaking or when planning what kind of car I want to purchase. For me, it's more than dreaming. I'm not just wishing—I'm actually there.

Even as a young entrepreneur, I believed in the power of visualization to make dreams come true. One day, when I was a twenty-nine-year-old living in Edmonton, I was flipping through a magazine and saw a picture of a Lear jet. I had never seen anything more beautiful in my entire life. I wanted that jet! When I looked at the picture of it, I visualized myself in it. I clipped out the picture and tacked it on my wall. Six years later I had a Lear jet!

YOU SAY I'M A DREAMER

Why are some people so adept at visualizing their dreams and turning those dreams into reality? In my experience, total dedication is crucial. Some people zigzag from impulse to impulse with no clear, consistent sense of purpose.

Motivational speaker and author Brian Tracy says, "All successful men and women are big dreamers. They imagine what their future could be, ideal in every respect, and then they work every day toward their distant vision, that goal or purpose."

Mark Victor Hansen, who co-created *Chicken Soup for the Soul* with Jack Canfield, told writer Mike Litman a remarkable story about the power of visualization:

> "First of all," he said, "you've got to figure out what you really want. In my case and in Jack's case, we didn't want a best-selling book. We wanted a MEGA best-selling book, *Chicken Soup for the Soul.* Beyond that, we didn't really want a best-selling book, we wanted to make a best-selling SERIES . . . We cut out the *New York Times* bestseller list. Then we put our names at the top before we ever got to the top in real life. Then we put it on my mirror, and we put one up at Jack's office, on his mirror . . . So in our mind's eye, when we were shaving, or the ladies were doing cosmetics, we owned the concept that we were best-selling authors before we actually were best selling."

In *Brainstorms and Thunderbolts* by Carol Madigan and Ann Elwood, King Gillette, who brought us the Gillette razor, wrote about his experience with visualization.

> As I stood there with the razor in my hand . . . the Gillette razor was born—more with the rapidity of a dream than by a process of reasoning. In that moment I saw

it all: the way the blade would be held in a holder; the idea of sharpening two opposite edges on a thin piece of steel; the clamping plates for the blade, with a handle halfway between the two edges of the blade. All this came more in pictures than conscious thought, as though the razor were already a finished thing and held before my eyes. I stood there before that mirror in a trance of joy...I could not foresee the trials and tribulations I was to pass through before the razor was a success. But I believed it with my whole heart.

Hollywood director Steven Spielberg once said, "I don't dream at night, I dream all day, I dream for a living." Like Spielberg, most successful people are incredible dreamers who know how to turn their dreams into reality.

BUILD SUCCESS THROUGH PASSION

When you feel passionately about achieving something, you move yourself closer to having it. Your passion drives success.

Roberta Bondar is best known as the first Canadian woman in space, but she is also a distinguished researcher in the field of neurology. As a child, Dr. Bondar had a passion for science. She loved chemistry sets and science fiction. She often imagined herself as part of the Flash Gordon stories, and explored her neighbourhood pretending to be an astronaut. She avidly followed the American space program through pictures and clippings sent to her by an aunt living in Florida. Roberta Bondar wanted to be a real astronaut one day.

In 1983, the National Research Council of Canada announced the formation of the Canadian space program and invited applications. Dr. Bondar was one of six people, chosen from more than four thousand applicants, who would begin training to become one of the first Canadian astronauts. She was the only female in the group. Beginning on January 22, 1992, she spent eight days in space on board Space Shuttle Discovery.

On her return to Earth, Dr. Bondar retired to devote time to her research and to photography. Inspired by her experiences in photographing Earth from space, she photographed all forty-one of Canada's national parks. The results were gathered into a book and museum exhibit, appropriately named *Passionate Vision*.

One of my heroes, Elvis Presley, formed his vision in part from comic books. "When I was a child," he said, "I was a dreamer. I read comic books, and I was the hero of the comic book. I saw movies, and I was the hero in the movie. So every dream I ever dreamed has come true a hundred times."

Take the time to visualize your future. Who will you be? Where will you be? Are you living your dreams?

CHAPTER 11

REHEARSE FOR SUCCESS

When I was appointed manager at First Investors Corp., my boss suggested I call a meeting of all my branches to establish a new regime. I decided we should all meet in Seattle at the Edgewater Inn. I'd never led a meeting before, so I arrived a day early to prepare. On the plane, I wrote each attendee's name on a place card.

When I got to the hotel, I went to the room where the meeting was to be held and placed the cards on the tables. Then I began to deliver my imaginary presentation. While I talked, I clearly imagined each attendee sitting in the room. One of them talked too much, so I moved his card. Another kept ganging up on me with the guy to his left. I moved his card, too. One guy never said anything, so I moved him closer to the front of the room to encourage him.

The next day, the meeting went off just as I had visualized it. It was one of the best presentations I have ever made.

ACT THE PART

To be successful, you must act the part. Get your life ready to receive success. Dress for it. Think positively. Associate with people you feel good about; think twice about hanging out with negative people. Be committed to your vision and stay focused on what you want to attract.

One evening, I met with Tom Hopkins, author of the bestselling book *How to Master the Art of Selling*. Over dinner and a glass of wine, our talk turned to motivation, and self-motivation in particular. I told Tom that I used to have a small index card hanging from my rearview mirror that said, "This is going to be the best presentation I have ever given!" I told him that looking at that card always worked for me.

"Well, that's pretty good," Tom said, "but here's what I used to do." He told me about standing in front of his mirror every morning, singing his own version of the Frankie Valli song, "Can't Take My Eyes Off of You." Tom's version went like this: "I'm just too good to be true, can't take my eyes off of me . . . ."

Maybe Tom was a little over the top, but he swears this singing strategy helped to motivate him. It's hard to argue with success.

"The people who are crazy enough to think they can change the world are the ones who do," says Steve Jobs, CEO of Apple Computers, so picture yourself living the life you want. Use the following exercises to develop your own visualization techniques; it is amazing what you will manifest.

VISUALIZE A GREAT DAY

What would a great day look like to you? Visualize a time in the near future and include key aspects of what you think would be a fabulous day—from beginning to end, from waking to the moment your head hits the pillow again at night. Where are you? What are you doing? Is it a workday or a day off? If you're dissatisfied with your professional situation, this would be a good time to envision a better one. Where would you work? What type of work would you do? Who would you have lunch with, and where? When would you head home? What would you eat for dinner? Where? Who would it be with? How would you spend your evening? Take a few minutes now and write down what your perfect day would look like.

VISUALIZE YOUR POTENTIAL

Let's take the visualization exercise mentioned earlier and apply it to your life in the longer term. Imagine yourself five years from now. Where are you and what are you doing? Who are the people in your life? Where do you live and with whom? What do you do with your time? What do you enjoy? Now imagine yourself ten years into the future. Ask yourself the same questions and imagine your life. Once you have done this, imagine your life twenty-five years from now. How will it be? Write a few paragraphs about what your life will look like in the future. Now, again, think about how to make it happen.

VISUALIZE "WHAT IF"

Michelangelo once wrote, "In every block of marble I see a statue as plain as though it stood before me, shaped and perfect in attitude and action. I have only to hew away at the rough walls that imprison the lovely apparition to reveal it to other eyes as mine see it." He did not see failure. What he saw were possibilities. What would you shape for your future if you knew you could not fail? What would you do if time and money were not factors? Explore a life of complete possibility. After all, what we visualize is real to our brains.

Remember my story of tacking a picture of the Lear jet to my wall, and then eventually owning one? That jet was so real to me that I could have flown in it right then and there. When I saw the picture of the Lear jet, I thought it was mine! When it actually became mine, all that really happened was my vision leapt out of my imagination and onto the tarmac.

I have no doubt that visualization works. But don't just take my word for it. Consider what Albert Einstein said: "Your imagination is a preview of life's coming attractions."

CHAPTER 12

FROM VISION TO ACTION

I feel you must take deliberate action to achieve your dreams. To say something like "I want to start my own profitable business" but walk around without setting plans into motion won't cut it. Look at well-known people in this world who are successful in their endeavours—they all have a strong sense of self-confidence and apply themselves at all costs to get what they want. Imagine if, after fifty tries, Thomas Edison had given up on that light bulb, or if Alexander Graham Bell had said, "forget this" as he was attempting to find new and improved ways to communicate. Edison, Ford, Gandhi, Martin Luther King, Bill Gates and Mother Teresa all had a vision for their lives and for the world and they were steadfast in their tenaciousness to make things happen. And they succeeded by taking action and never giving up.

Just as an artist paints a masterpiece one brushstroke at a time, accomplishing a goal involves more than stringing a series of actions together. Those actions do not have to be huge or sweeping; they can be baby steps you take one at a time. I learned this when I was just starting my career selling mutual funds. My manager, Lawrence Henniger, told me about the "18-3-1 Rule," which basically said I needed to make eighteen calls and deliver three presentations to make one sale. I decided that if that's what it would take for me to be successful, then that's what I'd do.

On the first day, I took eighteen paper clips from my desk and put them in the left pocket of my suit jacket. Each time I made a call, I moved a paper clip over to my right pocket. I told myself I couldn't go home until I had moved all the paper clips into my right-hand pocket. Was I successful at selling mutual funds? You bet. Taking even the smallest actions or breaking your goal down into bite-sized pieces is an important tool in creating your future.

IGNITE YOUR VISION

My friend Vince Poscente, who is an author and Olympian, knows all about turning a vision into action. At age twenty-six, he decided to take up speed skiing and pursue it competitively. Four years later, he raced for Canada in the 1992 Olympic Winter Games. How did he do it? Vince believes in the enormous potential of the unconscious mind. He took that belief one step further and decided to do what the competition wasn't willing to do, which was immerse himself in a great deal of mental training. Vince read every book he could get his hands on that discussed mental training strategies. He also participated in biofeedback exercises and hypnosis, and began using isolation tanks, also known as sensory deprivation tanks, to help him relax and meditate. "There were so many layers of mental training that I was able to turn it into a huge competitive advantage," Vince recalls. "Once you start doing what the competition isn't willing to do you discover stuff they haven't thought of. There's a domino effect of one idea to the next."

Vince has since written several books and dozens of articles on the power of the subconscious mind to help unlock human potential. In his book *The Ant and the Elephant*, Vince likens the dynamic between the conscious and subconscious minds to an ant and an elephant. The ant is the intentional, conscious part of the brain and the elephant is the impulsive subconscious. "While we tend to know our conscious minds, our ants, rather well, we often overlook the power of our elephantine subconscious minds," Vince says.

He believes the key is to get the ant and the elephant working together. "When you have the ant and the elephant headed in the same direction, you have a truckload of potential, rather than a spoonful," he says. Today Vince is an international speaker and consultant and the founder of Be

Invinceable Group, which helps people ignite their vision, execute their strategies and eclipse their competition.

Vince's wife, Michelle Lemmons-Poscente, founder of the International Speakers Bureau, is also a big believer in turning your vision into action. Since she started the firm in 1993, it has won numerous awards, including the Sprint #1 Small Business in America award in 2000. It was this award that eventually landed Michelle the starring role as head of her company in a Sprint television advertisement. But that coup didn't come easy, despite the award.

It was Michelle's idea to do the ad after her firm won the honour. When she told Sprint executives about the idea, they were keen and told her run it by their ad agency in New York. Michelle pitched it to the ad firm, but they didn't bite. She was not deterred. Instead of accepting no as the answer, Michelle continued to pursue her vision.

She went back to Sprint, who confirmed they still liked the concept. Sprint executives then arranged a meeting in Dallas between them, their New York ad firm and Michelle, in which she presented her idea again and turned that no into a yes. The ad aired months later, starring Michelle on the job.

Michelle says her strength always has been her ability to focus on her ultimate goal, no matter what obstacles might stand in the way. "To me, it's about seeing the end result and not just where I am right now. You can get paralyzed if you don't have the vision to see where you need to go," Michelle says. "You can't give up."

USE PROPS TO GET MOTIVATED

Another way to turn your vision into action is to identify any habits that might be holding you back. Try creating a list of behaviours you want to change. If you find yourself in need of motivation to break those habits, do whatever it takes to focus.

When I was immersed in some serious economic challenges (which I will tell you more about in the next chapter), I went out and bought a GI camouflage helmet and presented it to my lawyer. I needed him to concentrate completely on solving my considerable problems.

"If we're going to win this war," I told him, "we need to think 24/7 of our strategies. Losing isn't acceptable." John placed the helmet in a very prominent place in his office. We did win that war. It took as long as a real war—five years— but we did it. With the amount of focus we put on winning, there was no way we could lose.

If you ever find yourself in need of motivation to achieve your objectives, find whatever item you can to keep you and your team focused so the team members never forget how important their support is to you. Remember Tom Hopkins singing "I'm just too good to be true, can't take my eyes off of me"? That was his way of removing any negative thoughts and taking action. The reason there are winners and losers is because the winners turn their vision into action. To win, stay totally absorbed with the success of your objectives.

One of my favourite stories about the use of props to achieve a dream is about Jim Collins, author of *Good to Great*. Years ago, Collins, an avid climber, became obsessed with free-climbing Genesis, a "100-foot slab of red rock in Colorado's Eldorado Canyon." Free climbers rely on ropes only as the ultimate safety devices; they prefer to climb under their own power.

At that time, no one had ever free-climbed this rock—most people thought doing so was impossible. Collins felt he was strong, but Genesis intimidated him. He became determined to overcome his fear. In the book *Upward Bound: Nine Original Accounts of How Business Leaders Reached Their Summits*, Collins writes

In studying climbing history, I noticed a pattern: Climbs once considered "impossible" by one generation eventually became "not that hard" for climbers two generations later. . . . So, I decided to play a psychological trick on myself. I realized that I would never be the most gifted climber or the strongest climber or the boldest climber. But perhaps I could be the most futuristic climber. I did a little thought experiment. I tried to project out 15 years, and I asked myself, "What will Genesis seem like to climbers in the 1990s?" The answer came back clear as a bell. In the 1990s, the top climbers in the world would routinely on-site Genesis, viewing it as simply a warm up for even harder routes. And less-talented athletes would view Genesis as a worthy challenge, but hardly impossible. The barrier, I realized, was primarily psychological, not physical.

Collins embarked on an interesting exercise by projecting himself into the future, from 1979 to 1994. He bought a personal organizer and changed all of the dates in it to 1994. Then he visited the canyon and began to imagine Genesis the way a climber fifteen years into the future would see it.

"With that change in psychology," he writes, "I managed to climb through to the top of the route. It caused quite a sensation and confused many of the best climbers of the day. They were still climbing in 1979, whereas I had psychologically transported myself to 1994. And, indeed, by the early 1990s, these same elite climbers climbed Genesis routinely, no longer thinking of it as particularly hard. I watched one elite climber visiting from out of state walk to the base, nonchalantly rope up, climb flawlessly to the top, and lower down only to say, "Nice route"—and then amble off in search of stiffer stuff.

Collins' story shows how much power we actually have to achieve our goals. By changing his thinking, he changed the outcome. And sometimes, a simple prop such as a daily organizer can help turn a vision into action.

SEAL THE DEAL WITH AFFIRMATION

Now that you understand and appreciate the importance of visualization and techniques to help you live an extraordinary life, don't forget to give yourself a gift for working so hard. At the close of each day, congratulate yourself on what you have accomplished. Do not judge the size of your accomplishments; appreciate that you have moved your life forward. Feeling good about what you completed during your workday sets a positive foundation for your next day. Say to yourself, "I love my life and will create even greater success tomorrow."

We'll talk more about the gift of self-renewal and appreciating what you have in the coming chapters on inspiration and reflection.

FOUNDATION 4:

INSPIRATION

CHAPTER 13

THE GIFT OF
SELF-RENEWAL

In 1981, the North American real estate market tanked and my fortune of $150 million, which I had spent many years building, plunged almost overnight to *minus* $70 million. I was feeling pretty sorry for myself. If ever I needed a dose of inspiration, it was then. But I didn't wait for it to hit me like a bolt of lightning. Instead, I took action by checking in with my values.

As I described to you earlier in this book, I realized that I had many assets, even if money wasn't one of them. I was blessed with good health, a loving family and great friendships, as well as a strong work ethic and a solid reputation. This realization inspired me to pick myself up, dust myself off and move forward. When we saturate our minds with positive messages, as I did when the chips were down, we can transform our thinking and, in turn, our actions. Inspiration is like oxygen for the soul; all you have to do is breathe it in.

GET INSPIRED

Throughout history, men and women have had their personal inspirational rituals. Beethoven dumped ice water over his head. Brahms shined his own shoes. Kipling wrote with a certain type of black ink. Dickens slept with his bed pointing north (he believed the Earth's magnetic field stimulated him). You might not think you can stand pouring ice water over your head to spark inspiration; I don't think I can either. Fortunately, there are easier and more pleasurable ways to get inspired.

The trick is to find out what does it for you. In the book *Return on Imagination: Realizing the Power of Ideas*, authors Tom Wujec and Sandra Muscat wrote that

A creative mind-set for one person may be a state of anxiety for another. What stimulates a musician may bore a novelist. In fact, there isn't really a single state of mind — a combination of thoughts and moods — that we could call a creative mind-set. However, every person experiences peak moments when he or she is at a creative peak. Athletes call these peak moments the zone. Comedians call it being on a roll. Musicians call it getting in the groove. Psychologists call it flow or optimal experience.

There are innumerable ways to get inspired. How you do it isn't important, only that you find the best method for you. Here are a few tips that I hope will help you find your inspirational spark.

USE A NOTEBOOK

Sometimes we get inspirational thoughts and vow to commit them to memory. Unfortunately, these thoughts are often so ephemeral that they don't stay in our memories very long. Keep a small notebook with you and write down these thoughts as they occur. Look back over them whenever you need some inspiration. If writing isn't your thing, invest in a digital recorder and record your thoughts as they come up.

If a random idea comes to mind, don't dismiss it out of hand just because it doesn't fit with your standard view of the world. Write it down (or record it) and think about it. Be willing to clean out the stereotypes in your mind to make room for these wild ideas to take root. We think thousands of thoughts daily, and it stands to reason that some of them are the seed for inspiration.

You can find inspiration from pictures in books, newspapers and magazines. Cut them out and keep them where you can look at them on a regular basis, such as in a scrapbook or even folded away in your wallet. Sometimes these pictures will take you to places you find inspiring; sometimes they will fuel your dreams.

For example, if your dream is to visit Spain, collect travel brochures or guides that you can flip through when you want to feel inspired. Do you want to get in better shape? Find a picture of someone who you think looks fit. You get the idea. A woman I know spends every New Year's Day cutting out pictures of places she wants to visit during the coming year. She then pours some leftover eggnog and creates a collage of her travel dreams. She is no longer surprised when her visions become reality.

LIVE A LEARNING LIFESTYLE

Knowledge is the fuel for our inspiration. Unless you are continually learning new things, you really can't expect to be at your most creative and inspired.

Continual learning also keeps our brains limber as we age. It's the old "use it or lose it" axiom. At all costs we must avoid becoming like the juvenile sea squirt that Daniel C. Dennett describes in his book *Consciousness Explained*. According to Dennett, the sea squirt, with only a rudimentary nervous system, meanders through the ocean in search of the right rock or piece of coral to make its home in. When it finds the right spot, it takes root there. Since it doesn't need its brain any longer, it eats it. Unlike sea squirts, we need our brainpower throughout our lives, so we must keep using our brains.

Want proof that our brains need exercise just like the rest of our bodies? Studies have shown that people who play musical instruments tend to score better on tests in other areas such as math and languages. And a famous study done on elderly nuns showed they still had sharp minds thanks to being avid puzzlers! The research showed what those nuns actually were doing was creating connections in the neural pathways of their brains, something neurobiologists refer to as "use-dependent plasticity." Mental stimulation keeps you sharp even as you age. That's why it's a good idea to keep your mind limber, no matter what age you are. When you don't force your mind into new areas of exploration, you actually create ruts in your brain. Remember the old saying: "The only difference between a rut and a grave is the depth of the hole."

One of my favourite ways of keeping my brain active and inspired is to read everything I can get my hands on, including three or four newspapers a day, then put into practice the things I've learned that align with my values. Not only does reading exercise the brain, which is essential in staving off depression, it takes you on explorations into yourself. "A book," wrote Franz Kafka, "must be the axe for the frozen sea inside us."

My friend and mentor Jack Gilbert, a retired corporate lawyer and passionate photographer, is a testimony to life-long learning. Now in his early eighties, Jack is still working as a legal adviser in his hometown of Toronto. "Just because I'm officially 'retired' doesn't mean my legal mind goes soft," says Jack, who is always up to speed on the latest securities and corporate stories. Jack also shares his love for photography by teaching groups of his peers how to use Photoshop, a computer image-editing program. He loves that software because it never stops expanding and updating. "It's the same way I feel about life, there's always something new to learn."

Jack says he has an "open door policy" in life, which means he's open to talk to anyone about their story or ideas. "I find everyone has an interesting story to tell." He also travels worldwide. Of course, his vacations are always combined with seeking out business opportunities. "As long as I'm healthy, I don't want to retire. I find the world too exciting," says Jack. "There's too much going on."

COLOUR OUTSIDE THE LINES

Do things you've never done before, but always wanted to do, like taking an art class or learning how to skydive. I like to think of it as wringing the most out of life.

When I visualize the way I want to live my life, I picture myself taking a face cloth, dipping it in water, soaking up the water and squeezing every last drop of water out of the cloth. I want to experience everything. During my lifetime I've climbed the pyramids, driven a Formula 1 race car, jumped out of an airplane, flown a helicopter, crossed Alligator Alley in Florida on a jet boat, visited the Taj Mahal, scuba dived in

Fiji with just a rope separating me from the sharks, dived to 850 feet in a submarine, and raced motorcycles and Ferraris.

It's not just wild adventures that stimulate me. Whenever I see people really enjoying themselves, I want to find out why. In my view, the best way to do that is to experience it for myself.

Rita likes to tell the story about a ski trip we took to Sun Valley in central Idaho with some friends. We all were hanging out in the chalet before dinner when our friends took out a deck of cards and started playing a game. It was a ritual for them, something they did every night around that time for a bit of fun and relaxation. I turned to Rita and said, "Why don't we play cards every night?"

I decided right then to ensure we incorporated this into our daily schedule. Well, on our first day home we sat down and started to play cards. After less than five minutes I decided I would rather read. Hey, you know I had to try it!

Another way to bring some change to your life is to spend time with people outside your usual circle of friends, acquaintances and co-workers, perhaps by joining a social group or sports club. Ask these "outsiders" their opinions, especially if they know nothing about what you do in life.

By doing things you've never done before, whether it's taking an art class, playing cards or joining a club to meet new people, you are colouring outside the lines. This ensures you are creating your own masterpiece of life, rather than just filling in someone else's vision of what life should look like.

SWITCH GEARS

Meredith Thring, author of *How to Invent*, said an essential component of the creative state is a "switch" that turns off that niggling little critic in our mind that inhibits inspiration. Albert Einstein knew the power of doing this. Although he kept a regular work schedule, he also made time to switch off his "critical faculty" to take long walks on the beach or retreat to his bedroom so he could listen to what was happening inside his head. "If my work isn't going well," he said, "I lie down in the middle of a workday and gaze at the ceiling while I listen and visualize what goes on in my imagination."

Another way to switch gears is to take time out. One of my favourite stories about the benefits of taking time out involves two men splitting wood. One man was a 6-foot-6, 250-pound lumberjack in great physical shape. The other was a 130-pound nerd, all skin and bones. Both men began splitting wood at about the same time. They worked until coffee break, at which point the nerd quit splitting and took his break while the lumberjack just kept on splitting. The same thing happened at lunchtime, and again during the afternoon break. This went on for two weeks. The big lumberjack noticed that, despite his longer hours of work, he wasn't far ahead of the nerd. He worked extra hard into the nights, while the nerd left at six o'clock every evening. After three weeks of hard work, the lumberjack saw that the piles of split wood were about even between the two men.

By the end of the fourth week, it was really obvious the nerd had the advantage. One morning just before he left to have coffee, the lumberjack angrily accosted him. "I cannot understand why you have more wood split than I do," he sputtered. "You are smaller than I am, and you don't have the strength that I have." The nerd answered, "Ah yes, my friend, but you never stop to sharpen your axe!"

This story is a good reminder that we all need time off from work to think and refresh. Remember, you can only make so much money with your hands. How much you make with your brain is unlimited.

TRIGGER INSPIRATION

There are other methods of sparking inspiration, from personal triggers, to role models, to visiting places that bring back memories.

You've probably heard of a personal trigger. Many hypnotherapists use personal triggers to help their clients quit smoking, lose weight or reduce anxiety. A personal trigger is a biofeedback technique you can use to take you back to a time when you felt totally inspired or creative, in an effort to stimulate inspiration.

First, you must decide what personal trigger you want to use. Many people use the gesture of touching the index finger and thumb together. When you touch your fingers together, this acts as a physical signal or trigger that tells your mind it's time to return to a place of inspiration. The gesture you choose doesn't matter, but you might want to choose something you can do without embarrassment in a public place.

Now, relax and close your eyes. Think of a time when you felt particularly inspired. Try to fill the memory in with as much detail as you can. How did you feel when you were casting about for inspiration? What did it feel like when that "aha!" moment came to you? As soon as this memory and feeling crystallizes in you, touch your index finger and thumb together. Do this any time you want to recreate the feeling.

Another way to trigger inspiration is to model your thinking on people you find inspiring. How would they bring more inspiration and creativity into their lives? (Actually, this works with just about anything, not just inspiration.) When you imagine being that person and imitate their way of being, you communicate their talents to your subconscious. If you do this enough, the process becomes your own and their strengths become part of you, but you can't and shouldn't imitate another person forever.

In her book *The Artist's Way*, author Julia Cameron says some people find it easier to picture the stream of inspiration as being like radio waves. "With practice, we learn to hear the desired frequency on request. We tune in to the frequency we want. Like a parent, we learn to hear the voices of our current brainchild among the other children's voices."

Yet another way to trigger inspiration is to mentally revisit places where you spent your childhood, when you may have first formed those dreams you are pursuing today. I like to revisit some of mine now and again, sometimes with hilarious results.

I once ordered a massive bullwhip from an infomercial, much to Rita's surprise. When I was a kid growing up in a small town in Western Canada, I saw cowboys use these whips, and always had wanted to master the skill. After accidentally inflicting pain on myself, and a few household articles, I took my new hobby outside and eventually got the technique down pretty well, if you don't consider the damage to the flower garden.

FIND A GREAT SONG

As a big music lover, I also find inspiration in songs, especially if they are tied to a happy memory. Whenever I play Jennifer Rush's "The Power of Love," a song later covered by Céline Dion, immediately I am transported back to the first time I met Rita. This became our song. All of the love, laughter and emotion of young love comes back to me clearly each time I hear this song. When I play a song called "There Stands the Glass" by country musician Webb Pierce, I'm ten years old again, riding my bike home from school and singing at the top of my voice as I come over the hill.

And, whenever I hear "The Great Pretender" by Tony Williams and The Platters, I'm a sixteen-year-old in Alliston, Ontario, standing at a jukebox in a restaurant hanging out with my buddies. A lot of songs from the fifties and sixties remind me of a place called the Barr-X in Barrie, Ontario, where I would go as a teenager and dance all night long, never sitting down once. That also reminds me of Todd, who danced the same way. He would get up without a partner and dance the night away.

The fact that music so easily awakens our memories signals its power. Music boosts brainpower, affects focus, soothes senses, increases endurance and enhances creativity. We'll talk more about the power of music in the coming pages. Meantime, riffle through that old record collection and rediscover the inspirational power of a great song.

SET DEADLINES

If you are having trouble finding time to get inspired (and not even music will help) consider setting yourself a deadline. Some people feel they are at their most inspired when they are under pressure. From what we know about the effects of stress on the body, it's true that pressure may stimulate a temporary high that results in an inspired state. Many people need deadlines to stimulate inspiration and creativity. Novelist Rita Mae Brown says, "A deadline is negative inspiration. Still, it's better than no inspiration at all."

Do whatever works best for you, but don't wait for inspiration to hit you like a bolt of lightning. It's great when that happens, but some of the world's most inspired and successful people find ways to inspire themselves.

CHAPTER 14

RECOGNIZE
THE GENIUS WITHIN

The world is made up of ordinary people who do extraordinary things every day. Sometimes people tell me that I live an extraordinary life, but I know I'm not extraordinary. I'm just an ordinary guy who has ordinary fears and ordinary intelligence. I'm able to live an extraordinary life because I've tried to build my life on the Five Foundations I'm sharing with you in this book.

Many years ago, I was inspired by a book written by Glenn Clark called *The Man Who Tapped the Secrets of the Universe*. One particular piece of writing was life-changing: "I believe sincerely that every man has consummate genius within him. Some appear to have it more than others only because they are aware of it more than others are, and the awareness or unawareness of it is what makes each one of them into masters or holds them down to mediocrity."

At the moment I read that passage, I realized I had genius within me and it was up to me to uncover it, not wait for other people to find it. My success, or lack of it, was my choice and no one else's. *I was the one who could make anything happen by believing in myself and staying focused on goals that aligned with my values. I was in charge of my life.*

If you have learned to hide your light and reject new ideas, it's time to take a deep look at the person you really are—the genius who was born with potential and the spirit to realize your dreams. The root of the word "genius" is the Latin word that means "spirit." Take a moment to ask yourself, "What would my life be like if I allowed the spirit of my inner genius to shine?"

THINK OUTSIDE THE BOX

So often, we look at people who are considered to be geniuses and wonder what they have that we don't have. From what I've seen, most geniuses, instead of accepting the status quo, learn how to think outside the box. They take things out of that box and turn them around, upside down and inside out. From the most successful entrepreneurs to the greatest scientists, this ability to look at life from new angles is what results in those "aha!" moments we associate with genius.

Leonardo da Vinci believed this. He advocated always looking at problems and dilemmas from several different perspectives. For instance, by seeking commonalities in the relationship between the ring of a bell and a stone hitting water, he discovered that sound travels in waves.

Einstein always formulated his theories in as many different ways as possible. While other scientists used mathematical formulas to reach their conclusions, Einstein—a known visual thinker—often drew pictures and diagrams. Numbers did not play a significant role in his thinking process.

You may feel you need an IQ like Einstein's to be a genius, but according to Dr. Martin Brooks there seems to be "no single recipe" for genius. High IQ doesn't always predict genius, nor does academic achievement. "Genius, it seems, demands the expression of qualities often denied by traditional schooling and intelligence tests," Dr. Brooks says. "Though exceptional ability may be a key ingredient, you must also throw courage and creativity into the mix. Top that off with a talent for visualizing problems from new and original angles, and you may be getting somewhere toward that elusive formula."

To illustrate his point, Dr. Brooks refers to the case of Tony DeBlois, a musician who could play twenty instruments and had more than eight thousand songs committed to memory. DeBlois suffered from a form of autism known as savant syndrome. People with this syndrome often have exceptional abilities in one area but remarkable deficiencies in another. In other words, it's not what you've got—it's what you do with it.

In 1921, Dr. Lewis Terman of Stanford University launched a decades-long study of 1,500 children who had IQs above the genius level. He wanted to find the correlation between IQ and success. Like Dr. Brooks, he discovered IQ was not the most vital component of success. The real success factors, he found, were self-confidence, perseverance and the ability to set goals—components of what is known as "emotional intelligence."

TURN ON YOUR "POSSIBILITY RADAR"

Finding the confidence to create the life you want often means stepping back and looking at the possibilities around you, rather than staying in situations that make you unhappy, unhealthy or both. The following story, often told by inspirational speaker John Assaraf, mentioned earlier in this book, is a good example of the need to do this. One day a man walked into a room and noticed a fly buzzing frantically against a windowpane. When the man looked again in ten minutes, the fly was still buzzing away at the window. Three hours later, he walked by the window again and the fly was gone. He looked down and saw about a dozen flies lying dead on the window ledge. He then looked up to see, only a few feet away, an open window.

Some of us spend a lot of our lives trying to pursue dreams and objectives by "buzzing" against the window of life. We see our goals in front of us and believe if we just buzz harder and longer we'll be rewarded. In fact, we should stop our frantic "buzzing," back up and look around for another opening.

Stepping back to get perspective was exactly what Kumar Shivdasani, a physician at Vancouver General Hospital, did after attending one of my LifePilot workshops. "I've been blessed by a number of wonderful experiences," Kumar says. "Opportunities have come into my life that I recognized as 'opportunities' because they touched and connected with my values, strengths, and in some ways even what I perceived as weaknesses . . . I've been able to face many of my fears and overcome those obstacles of, 'oh no, I can't do that!' As a result of walking through my fears, I've done a list of things my mind said I couldn't do: half-marathons and eventually a full marathon, triathlons, and climbing the tallest peak outside of the Himalayas—Mt. Aconcagua (almost 23,000 feet)."

Inspired by the possibilities he now saw in his life, Kumar went on to climb another of the Seven Summits—:Mt. Elbrus in Russia, the tallest peak in Europe. He also became involved in a charity devoted to raising money for children's health initiatives. Kumar found the courage to create the life he really wanted.

TAP INTO YOUR POTENTIAL

The Japanese-American artist Isamu Noguchi, considered one of the great sculptors of the twentieth century, credited his mother with helping him to believe in his talent. By all accounts, she was a strong and powerful influence on his early development, just as my mother was in my life. We should all be so fortunate as to have such strong champions of our potential. But whether you do or don't have support for your talents, you must look inside and recognize the potential you possess. It's still there, no matter what your age.

Rediscovering your talents is an amazing process, a bit like searching for a long-lost treasure you buried as a child. When you find it, you'll remember how good it felt, and how right.

Steven Funk, a former colleague of mine, dreamed of becoming a farmer. But somehow the Iowa farm kid ended up pursuing an education in oral surgery. It wasn't until he was well into his post-secondary education that he realized he was moving toward a destination that didn't excite him.

So why did Steven choose a career in oral surgery? "I remember jumping up and down on the bed when I was a little kid," he says. "My dad was there and he was asking, 'What are you going to be when you grow up?' I said, 'Dad, I'm going to be a farmer'—because my dad was a farmer. I remember him saying, 'You don't want to be a farmer. Go be a doctor.' "

He did what his father wanted him to do. He studied at the University of Iowa in his home state, and then moved to Vancouver for his residency—a city he picked after reading a *National Geographic* magazine.

Steven tried to find something about a career in oral surgery that appealed to him, but his heart wasn't in it. He remembers returning to Iowa for Christmas one year, and talking to a friend from dental school about how they hated the job and couldn't wait to retire. Steven said the thought of an Iowa farm boy with a love of the outdoors spending the rest of his working life cooped up in an office was unbearable. He wanted to live more of a freelance lifestyle.

Uncertain about the future, Steven returned to Vancouver, where I eventually met him. In fact, my business partner and I hired him. One moment he was an oral surgery resident, the next he was working for two fast-moving entrepreneurs whose entire approach to life was full of enthusiasm—and anything but 9 to 5. It was the freelance life he'd dreamed about back in school. Steven went on to become founder and chairman of a major corporation. And true to his farming background, he now oversees nearly one hundred thousand acres of precious sustainable development and environmental custodianship in the rainforest of Belize. He also owns agricultural farmland with his family in Iowa.

Like so many people, Steven had a potential and a calling he almost denied. Although Steven's father undoubtedly wanted the very best for his son, the father's dream wasn't

Steven's dream. By looking deep inside, Steven found the courage to pursue his dream and turn it into a success.

When I think of people like Kumar and Steven I'm reminded of what theologian Carl Bard said: "Though no one can go back and make a brand new start, anyone can start from now and make a brand new ending."

Don't wait to feel like a genius before you set off on a journey to a more fulfilling life. The time to act is now. You have what you need. It's time to believe in yourself and get your ideas off the ground.

CHAPTER 15

It's Not What You Have, It's Who You Have

I started my first company when I was twenty-eight years old. My lawyer advised me that I needed to appoint some directors who could give my young company the wisdom, direction and strategic advice it needed to grow. But I was so young that I had not met people who could supply the advice and guidance I needed. So I improvised.

I owned a book of black and white portraits taken by the famous Yousuf Karsch, which included photographs of John F. Kennedy, Martin Luther King Jr., Ernest Hemingway, Gandhi, and others. I cut their pictures out of the book, framed them and hung them in my office. These were men of distinction, with much wisdom, and so I appointed them as my board of directors.

As my business faced challenges, I would ask each one of them what they would do about a particular kind of issue.

JFK was my business advisor; MLK my arbiter on what was right and wrong; Gandhi my spiritual guide; and Hemingway—well, he gave me permission to have a little fun. They were my mentors, albeit virtual.

Whether virtual or living, mentors are important. There's nothing like having people around who have the gifts, abilities and wisdom to complement you and provide reassurance when you're facing challenges. Mentors have played significant and dramatic roles in shaping my life and my business. Mostly, these people have been generous, kind, honest, helpful and supportive—true advocates who encouraged me to go for my goals and stretched me to reach them.

Sure, you can succeed on your own. I suppose it depends on what success looks like to you. But the support, encouragement and love of the people in your life are absolutely vital to success in the nth degree.

DISCOVER THE MAGIC OF MENTORSHIP

Mentoring is one of the oldest forms of influence. Through the ages, successful men and women have experienced the power of mentorship to gain knowledge. They have relied on mentors to help open important doors to the future.

Our culture is filled with stories of famous mentoring relationships, both factual and fictitious. Scholars have noted that mentors were commonplace in Africa, long before the beginnings of ancient Greek civilization. But it wasn't until Homer's fictional Roman character Odysseus, the hero of the Trojan Wars, came along that mentoring had a formal name in Western civilization. In Homer's *The Odyssey*, Odysseus had a wise teacher whose name was said to be Mentor. According to myth, the goddess Athena would take on Mentor's form for the purpose of giving counsel. When Odysseus left on his travels, he entrusted the care of his son, Telemachus, to Mentor. From that point on, Mentor's name came to depict a wise and trusted counsellor.

The story of King Arthur and Merlin is another classic example of a mentoring relationship that came from historical fiction. When Arthur was just a boy, Merlin became his mentor and helped him develop his strengths. Merlin also arranged opportunities for Arthur to secure the kingship, including the challenge of the sword in the stone. Later, Merlin created the legendary round table by which Arthur governed.

The mentoring relationship is the basis of Mitch Albom's book *Tuesdays with Morrie*, about his relationship with his old college professor Morrie Schwartz. When Albom found out that Schwartz was dying of Lou Gehrig's disease, he reunited with his professor and met with him every Tuesday to discuss everything from work to forgiveness to love. There are many other such famous relationships. Frodo had Gandalf, Alexander the Great had Aristotle, Jung had Freud,

Gail Sheehy had Margaret Mead, and Helen Keller had Anne Sullivan. Most of us can identify someone who has had a positive, significant impact on our lives.

Mentors can be friends, relatives, co-workers and teachers, as well as historic or contemporary personalities. Most often, a mentor is a more experienced or older person who acts as a role model, compatriot, challenger, guide or cheerleader.

Writer Thomas Wolfe's mentor not only made him feel he could become great; he was there when greatness seemed a long way off. "I was sustained by one piece of inestimable good fortune," says Wolfe. "I had for a friend a man of immense and patient wisdom and a gentle but unyielding fortitude. I think that if I was not destroyed at this time by the sense of hopelessness that this gigantic labour has awakened in me, it was largely because of the courage and patience of this man. I did not give in because he would not let me give in."

CHOOSE YOUR MENTORS

You have heard about my virtual mentors, from JFK to Hemingway. Virtual mentors can help you access the wisdom of the ages. To identify and learn about your virtual mentors, comb the Internet, bookstores or libraries for biographies of people you admire. Learn how they conquered their challenges. Try to identify the key things they did to achieve their dreams. The more you learn about your virtual mentors, the more wisdom you will draw from them.

While virtual mentors will sustain you through many of life's challenges, you should also try to find people with whom you can have regular human contact. I recommend that, in addition to your virtual board of directors, you identify five people you would like to mentor you.

One of my mentors is Ken Marlin, who was my general manager at First Investors Corporation, a company he helped found and grow. After leaving First Investors, Ken started Marlin Travel in a basement office in Edmonton. The business blossomed to 320 agencies and became Canada's best-known travel brand before it was sold to Thomas Cook Travel in 1998. Through the years, Ken has been very generous in sharing his time and wisdom with me. He gets a real thrill out of motivating people to achieve their potential.

Ken credits his mother for giving him this skill. The 1920s were very tough economic years and by age twelve, Ken was working hard. "I didn't think I was just a kid," he remembers. Then Ken's dad died when Ken was fifteen. His mother took charge and Ken learned from her "management style," which he later passed on to his employees and the people he mentored.

"She had the ability to direct us without being bossy," he recalls. "She explained and motivated us to do what needed to be done."

Ken has led a fascinating and diverse life. The knowledge he passes on to me doesn't just come from a boardroom; it comes from his work in the fields, as a telegrapher on the railways (he learned Morse code and still talks to other telegraphers in Morse today), as a house builder and as an outstanding salesperson. He sold refrigerators and vacuums door-to-door for Electrolux (yes, Electrolux once sold refrigerators) and learned a host of sales strategies.

Ken met Stan Melton, Ralph Forrester and Don Cormie as the three were about to form a "little company" called First Investors Corporation. Anyone who knows Ken knows First Investors might never have become the success it did, without his hard work and innovative input. He credits his success at First Investors to his almost crusade-like belief that people can achieve financial freedom by learning to save money. He firmly believes in the words of James J. Hill, founder of the Great Northern Railway: "The test is simple and infallible. Are you able to save money? If so, the seed of success is in you."

He set a goal to become a millionaire by age forty and achieved his goal. When I went to work at First Investors and met Ken, I took to him right away. He taught me so many things, including how to set goals, stay focused and channel my enthusiasm into results.

Ken is always available to me. He loves to tell the story of the day I barged through the door of his house at 6 a.m. like I owned the place. "I was in the bathroom shaving,"

Ken recalls. "Peter just came right in, sat down on the toilet seat and made himself at home. He had some new idea—he always had ideas—and he was going to tell me that idea no matter what time it was." I remember that Ken's wife, Helen, came into the bathroom and asked me if I could put my idea on hold while Ken finished shaving.

Instead of telling me what to do while on the job, Ken would encourage me to come up with my own answers. At one point, I was sent to another city to investigate why the office there wasn't making money and why some funds were mysteriously missing. After investigating, I decided to fire the manager. My next move was to tell Ken what I had done to solve the problem.

"So, now what are you going to do?" Ken asked. He made sure I knew I wasn't going anywhere until a new manager was found. It took me three months, but I solved the problem. In allowing me the space to tackle this problem on my own, and to see it through, Ken taught me lessons that still influence me today.

Now in his eighties, Ken is still full of energy and devotes himself to mentoring and teaching the Marlin Method of investing and financial management to rising executives and entrepreneurs.

Just as Ken and I had similar values and goals, your mentors should share your values and possess qualities or areas of expertise you would like to see in yourself. When it comes to your career, I recommend you choose mentors that are about fifteen years older than you. This allows for enough of an age difference that competition and ego are not issues. Another advantage of selecting older mentors is they have already navigated many of the aspects of life you are now just beginning to explore. Your mentors should not be in competition with you or need anything you've got.

A mentoring relationship should be positive. Mark Twain advised, "Keep away from people who try to belittle your ambitions. Small people always do that, but the really great make you feel that you, too, can become great."

That doesn't mean a mentor should always be gentle. "The dream," says retired television anchor Dan Rather, "begins with a teacher who believes in you, who tugs and pushes and leads you to the next plateau, sometimes poking you with a sharp stick called 'truth.'"

Your mentors should also be people you respect and with whom you can talk openly. They should be willing to share their networks with you, and have time to spend with you.

Remember that not every mentoring relationship is forever. Sometimes, people have an important role to play in your life for only a set period of time. Some mentors come into your life only for a very short time and teach you lessons that stay with you. Be grateful for what you have learned and let your mentors know how much you appreciate what they have offered you.

Finally, not every mentor can address every area of your life. I have had mentors for various areas of my life: in business, in fitness and even in my love of Harley-Davidson motorcycles.

Rita initially had a difficult time choosing her mentors. She couldn't think of anyone she wanted to emulate. "It took me some time to realize you can pick a mentor based on what they excel at because no one is perfect," Rita recalls.

Now her list of mentors seems endless. She loves looking up to people who know a lot more about some of her passions than she does, and are willing to share their experiences.

For Rita, her mother is her inspirational mentor. Rita's mother goes to church every day, exercises six days a week, is very careful about what she eats, and hugs everybody she can. Now in her late eighties, Rita's mother has no aches and pains and more energy than most fifty-year-olds. She lives a life based on love.

"Who wouldn't want to be just like her?" Rita says.

Rita's sister is her spiritual advisor and her grandson Trent is her "see life through a child's eye" mentor. Rita has mentors to keep her positive, to help her eat well, and even a travel mentor.

Who are the people that inspire you? What do you want to learn from them? As you can see from Rita's mentors, you may need or want all kinds of mentors in your life for the diversity of wisdom they can offer you.

LEARN THE ROPES

My friend Alfredo J. Molina, whom you met earlier in the book, drew on the wisdom of virtual mentors as he built Molina Fine Jewelers in Phoenix. For mentors, he looked to jewellery icons like Winston, Cartier, Fabergé and Tiffany. Alfredo would ask himself, "What would Harry Winston do in this situation?"

"I still refer to my virtual mentors today," says Alfredo, "and you know, it's funny, even the people around me know about this. One time I was on a phone call and had to make a decision. My public relations assistant was in the room. When I got off the phone, she asked me, 'Would Harry Winston do this?'"

One of my favourite stories about Alfredo involves Harry Winston. Winston was known as the king of diamonds. He loved diamonds so much he always carried one with him. People came to expect this from him, and often, at parties and other gatherings, they would come over to see which diamond he happened to be carrying that day.

Alfredo and I were in Beverly Hills one day, walking down Rodeo Drive. We ran into another jeweller Alfredo knew and stopped to chat with him in his store. To my surprise, Alfredo pulled out of his pocket the 76.45-carat Archduke Joseph Diamond named for the Archduke of Austria. At the time, this diamond was the twelfth-largest perfect white diamond in the world, and there was Alfredo showing it to his associate in a Beverly Hills store.

I couldn't believe it, and asked my friend why he did that. Ten minutes later, we went to another jeweller's shop, where a prince of Saudi Arabia walked in looking for something unique. Alfredo just happened to have this stone in his pocket and showed the prince. While no sale was made that day, Alfredo was able to meet the prince and make a valuable connection.

"Peter was shocked," Alfredo recalls of that day. "Ten minutes earlier he had been telling me how silly I was!"

From a virtual mentor like Harry Winston, Alfredo had learned, among other things, to always be ready for opportunity.

MEET YOUR MENTORS

Many successful people are willing to act as mentors. It is their way of giving back some of the generous advice they've received on their paths to success. They know what it's like to start out, and they are willing to share their knowledge. The best will also share their networks. Some mentoring relationships develop almost organically, but when that avenue isn't open to you, one of the best ways to find a mentor is by looking around at people you admire.

Check your network. Is there someone you've met who you would like to learn from? Many organizations link retired professionals with people seeking mentorship. Chambers of commerce and boards of trade may offer this as part of their membership benefits packages. Groups such as the Entrepreneurs' Organization and the Young Presidents' Organization also offer valuable mentorship programs.

My advice is to request a meeting with your mentor of choice and ask if he or she would consider mentoring you. Tailor the delivery and detail of your proposal to how well you know the person. Tell them why you chose them and what you hope to gain. Be clear about your focus so they can be clear about what they can honestly contribute. As with most proposals, the worst they can say is no. Even then, they'll likely be flattered.

Remember, mentoring is a give-and-take relationship. It's important to be an active participant in the process, to come to your meetings prepared and to follow up on what you and your mentor discussed. When you can, find opportunities to contribute value to your mentors.

"Successful people are always looking for opportunities to help others," says motivational expert Brian Tracy. "Unsuccessful people are always asking, 'What's in it for me?'"

BEING A MENTOR YOURSELF

Winston Churchill once said, "We make a living by what we get, but we make a life by what we give." This quote perfectly captures the attitudes of most people who decide to share their knowledge by mentoring. Mentorship is helping someone else by sharing your experience and connections.

One of my greatest pleasures has been to mentor others and give back something of what I've experienced. For example, I love to participate in The Global Student Entrepreneur Awards (GSEA) program, which honours undergraduate students that own and run businesses while attending a college or university. In 2008 I was chair of the judging committee. It's one of many ways I like to mentor and share my experiences, and what I hope is some valuable advice.

Mentoring also helps me reflect on my life and what I've learned. Rather than deplete my energy, I find mentoring to be very energizing. Not only do I pass along my knowledge, I also learn from the person I am mentoring.

In this regard, I think of these words of Buddha: "Thousands of candles can be lighted from a single candle and the life of the candle will not be shortened." While I no longer have time for a great deal of one-on-one mentoring, my way of giving back is through books like this and through my LifePilot workshops delivered around the world.

In my experience, being a good mentor requires interest, patience and time, and the confidence within that you have something to offer. Most importantly, you need to do it because you are sincerely interested in helping another person reach his or her goals. Helping others achieve success brings satisfying personal rewards and leaves a lasting legacy. The more you reach out and help others, the more success will come back to you.

CHAPTER 16

IF YOU NEVER QUIT, YOU NEVER FAIL

One day, when I was a boy, I was riding a horse at full gallop along a trail I had taken many times before. I knew the trail and so did the horse. We were approaching a fork in the road, and my gaze was straight ahead. I did not anticipate the actions of the horse; for some reason it veered abruptly at the fork. I lost control of the reins and fell from the saddle, hitting the ground so hard that I lost consciousness. When I came to, some of the other kids were standing over me. They helped me to my feet and we went off to catch my horse.

Sometimes in life you will find yourself tearing straight ahead with your plans set, when all of a sudden life makes a right turn for no apparent reason, just as my horse had done. When you fall, as you often will, you've got to pick yourself up and get back at it immediately. It doesn't matter why life turned right or left or whose fault it is. Accept the facts, pick yourself up and get back in the saddle. If you never quit, you never fail. The true sign of a winner is the ability to bounce back after a defeat.

You will only fail when you give in before you've done all you can to make something a success. Robert F. Kennedy once said, "Only those who dare to fail greatly can ever achieve greatly." Most people are so afraid of taking risks that they avoid anything in which they could fail. In my opinion, they are cowards.

If you study the background of any successful person, you will probably unearth a string of mistakes, rejections and disappointments. It's called paying your dues. You will also generally find that they have tried more and worked harder to achieve their goals than others have. They get the law of averages to work for them.

Here are some examples:

- Barbara Walters was told by Don Hewitt, who later became the producer of *60 Minutes*, to "stay out of television." She became one of the most famous women on T.V anyway.
- Steven Spielberg's mediocre grades meant he could not get into UCLA's film school. He made *ET* and *Close Encounters* anyway.

- John Grisham's first novel, *A Time to Kill*, was rejected by sixteen agents and twelve publishers. He became a bestselling author anyway.
- The Beatles were rejected by Decca Records in 1962. They became the world's most famous rock band anyway.
- Elvis Presley's music teacher in Memphis told him he couldn't carry a tune. He became "the King" anyway.
- Billy Crystal was chosen as an original cast member for *Saturday Night Live* but was cut from the cast before the first show aired. He went on to star in highly successful comedies anyway.

THERE'S NO STRAIGHT LINE TO ACHIEVEMENT

Achieving your goals won't always be easy. Sometimes you will have to deal with setbacks, but with a positive attitude you will move forward, just as inventor Thomas Edison did when his laboratory in New Jersey burned down in 1914. He lost more than two million dollars' worth of equipment and research. The next day, the inventor toured the site and poked through the ashes. "There is great value in disaster," he said. "All our mistakes are burned up. Thank God we can start anew." Edison easily could have closed his doors forever, but he chose to take a positive view of an otherwise disastrous situation. He didn't lose sight of his goals, and neither should you. No matter what, remain optimistic and undeterred. Keep moving forward.

The great Irish writer James Joyce said, "A person's errors are his portals of discovery." I've been through plenty of portals of discovery. However, I realized a long time ago that making mistakes or falling on hard times isn't a problem in life; it's a natural part of the whole process of learning and growth. How we deal with it is what separates the self-defined winners and losers. One of my favourite quotes is from Will Rogers, who said, "You've got to go out on a limb sometimes because that's where the fruit is."

When it seems like the odds are stacked against you, it might also be helpful to think about the story of a farmer whose old horse fell down a well. The poor horse neighed for hours as the farmer mulled over how to get it out. Finally, the farmer reasoned that the horse was old and the well needed to be covered up anyway. He invited his neighbours to help him shovel dirt into the well. When the horse saw this, he began to neigh again. Then, to everyone's amazement, he quieted down. A few shovel loads later, the farmer finally looked down into the well and was astonished by what he saw. With every shovelful of dirt that landed on top of the animal, he would shake it off and take a step up. After a few hours, the horse stepped up over the edge of the well and trotted away. Sometimes life shovels a lot of dirt on you along the path to achieving your goals. It's important not to give up. Shake off the dirt and step up to your future.

DISMISS NAYSAYERS

If someone tells me I can't, I take it as a dare, because I know I can. I could never see imposing limitations or restrictions on myself. I'm a possibility thinker. We are thinking, feeling human beings who get hurt when bad things happen. But we do have much more control over our destiny than most of us think. We can stretch to our maximum potential, and we can achieve whatever we want to in life if we focus on the possibilities—not the limitations—and what can be done through belief in ourselves, our abilities and the people around us.

Catherine Crier, a television broadcaster, author, lawyer and former judge, dealt with naysayers for most of her early career. It started when she was in law school, when female lawyers were not as common a sight, and built up when she decided at age twenty-eight to run for the bench. "I heard over and over again that I was too young, too inexperienced, and that it was an inappropriate place for me," Catherine recalls. It didn't stop her. At age thirty she became the youngest state judge ever to be elected in Texas. Shortly after her unopposed re-election, she had a chance meeting with a TV executive and decided to take what she calls "a 90-degree career turn." She was hired to co-anchor the premiere evening newscast on CNN. She recalls the media coverage: "There was a huge uproar. I remember reading a story that said an actress and model was hired at CNN. It wasn't until further down in the story did it say that I was a lawyer and a judge. That is the way they treated my transition, rather than respect my qualifications."

How did she cope? "There were times you closed the door and cried. Then you would just suck it up, and take a deep breath," says Catherine, describing herself as "skeptical, pragmatic, optimistic, idealist."

She went on to anchor high-profile programs at ABC News, the Fox News Channel and Court TV before branching out on her own. Today Catherine is a managing partner in Cajole Entertainment, developing television, film and documentary projects.

Catherine says she pressed on back then, despite those who said she couldn't, or criticized her career moves. "As a little girl, my parents would tell me, 'There is no such thing as can't.' That was a pretty powerful thought for a child." Years later, she moderated a seminar titled "Courage to risk—Freedom to fail." Catherine says those two statements sum up her personal attitudes about challenges in life. "If you give yourself permission to fail, if that is not the end of the line, you will do all sorts of things because you can take risks and make changes." Today, Catherine says she has very little fear of failure.

"You can't get distracted when people tell you that your idea is stupid and isn't going to work," advises Amazon founder and CEO Jeff Bezos. "Invention always leads you down a path that people are going to think is weird."

According to Bezos, successful entrepreneurs confront criticism and failure with "a unique combination of stubbornness and flexibility."

People will always criticize risk takers. In his 1910 speech in Paris, Theodore Roosevelt said, "It is not the critic who counts, nor the man who points out how the strongman stumbled, or where the doer of deeds could have done better. The credit belongs to the man who is actually in the arena, whose face is marred with dust and sweat and blood, who strives valiantly, who errs and comes up short again and again, who knows great enthusiasms, great devotions, and spends himself in a worthy cause, who at best knows achievement and who at worst if he fails at least fails while daring greatly so that his place shall never be with those cold and timid souls who knew neither victory nor defeat."

During LifePilot workshops, I like to ask participants to guess who the following person is. See if you can figure it out:

He had to work to support his family after they were forced out of their home.
His mother died.
He failed in business.

He was defeated in his bid for the legislature.

He lost his job and couldn't get into law school.

He declared bankruptcy, and spent the next seventeen years of his life paying off his debts.

He borrowed from friends to start his business.

He was defeated again in his bid for the legislature.

His fiancé died and his heart was broken.

He had a nervous breakdown and spent the next six months in bed.

He was defeated in his bid to become the speaker of the state legislature.

He was defeated in becoming an elector.

He was defeated in his bid for Congress.

He was defeated again in his bid for Congress.

He was defeated yet again in his bid for Congress.

He was rejected for a job.

He was defeated in his bid for the Senate.

He was defeated in his bid for Vice-President and got fewer than one hundred votes.

He was defeated again in his bid for the Senate.

He was elected President of the United States.

Most people find it hard to believe that this long saga of so-called failures is actually a blow-by-blow account of the life of Abraham Lincoln, the sixteenth president of the United States.

DARE GREATLY, BUT
DO YOUR HOMEWORK

I take risks, but like most successful risk takers I've learned the value of combining risk with research. When I was negotiating the Century 21 Real Estate franchise rights for Canada, I took a risk that turned out to be one of the best financial moves I've ever made.

We had finished our negotiating and planned to reconvene the next day to conclude the transaction. That evening, I tried to work out the numbers to see just how good this investment really could be. Century 21 had a regional franchise agreement that the mother company used with every group of investors around the world. I felt I could not afford to pay them as much as the other regions because my region was different, but how could I explain that and still acquire the rights to what I felt would be the best deal I had ever done?

I loved the project but decided there should be an accommodation for the unique geography of Canada. The next day, I explained to the group that Canada was a very big country—actually bigger than the continental United States. I argued that because of the size of the region, it would be so much more expensive to provide proper and professional service to our clients that we could not afford to pay the same fees paid by other investor groups whose clients were not spread so thinly over a large geographic area.

The Century 21 principals bought the argument and I received a one-third discount on the fees to compensate for the size of the country. My high-risk investment of $5,000 became a business that would generate billions of dollars in sales a year. Many years later, when Century 21 Canada sold, its value was substantially more than any other region in the company system.

A lot of the reason for the high value was the extraordinary job done by the management and staff, but it also had much to do with the fact that the discount I negotiated left more on our bottom line and increased our value substantially.

When I first looked at the opportunity to acquire the rights for the franchise, my business partners all had very valid opinions about why it would not work, but none of these opinions were based on facts. I felt I had done my due diligence and had covered all of my questions so, based on my instincts, I went ahead with the acquisition of the Canadian rights. The rest, as they say, is history.

If you feel strongly about an issue and know that you have done your homework, trust your instincts and dare greatly. People love to romanticize about risk takers, so go ahead and let them, as long as you know the facts and exactly what is at risk.

One story that always reminds me to look at the whole picture is the tale of three blind men who were led up to an elephant and asked to determine what an elephant looked like. One of the blind men approached the elephant from the front and came into contact with its trunk. He said, "An elephant is long and skinny like a snake." The next blind man approached the elephant from the side. He reached up under the elephant and touched its belly. "The elephant is like some large balloon that floats in the air," he said. The third blind man approached the elephant from the back and put his arms around the elephant's hind leg. "The elephant is a creature that is built like a pillar reaching up to the sky," he said.

Each man had a totally different view of what an elephant looked like. They were all partially correct but none of them had the full picture. The next time you need to make a decision, ask yourself if you have explored the entire elephant.

KNOW WHEN TO CUT YOUR LOSSES

I've said the only time you fail is when you quit, but when you've done your utmost and nothing seems to be working, sometimes you have to cut your losses.

Many people, when they find themselves going down the wrong road, have a tendency to try and go faster. But increasing your speed isn't going to get you moving in the right direction. You need to stop, turn around and reassess your aims.

Once, I was part of a home construction project that just kept going from bad to worse. Even so, we kept putting in more money. Finally, we had to stop and really consider where we stood. It appeared that if we kept funding the project, we could lose a lot more money than we already had. If we cut our losses and changed contractors, it would be difficult and would cost us a lot of money, but the upside was that we could bring on board a new contractor who would be bonded. We would be guaranteed no more losses. We chose to change contractors. Many issues in life are like that.

If a situation or a deal is bad, the first loss is usually the cheapest loss. Take it and move on. Learn from what you've experienced, but don't be afraid to ever risk again.

KEEP SMILING

It's easy to become discouraged when the path to our goals isn't a straight runway to success. But many successful people will tell you their characters were built as much by their so-called failures as by their successes.

I, too, know the power of hard work and persistence. When I was twenty-eight years old and just beginning my career, I was appointed as a first-time manager. Now I had to count on my ability to get results from others rather than just doing it myself. On a particularly worrisome day, I shared some of my frustrations with my boss, Ken Marlin. He listened patiently then said some simple and powerful words I've never forgotten: "Peter, keep smiling and leaning."

No matter how bad a day you're having, or how many things seem to drive you away from your pre-set objectives, just keep your head down and plough ahead. With your values identified and your goals set out, you'll be surprised how well you can operate.

Dale Carnegie was known for his ability to "shut the door on the past with so resolute a slam and with hardly a backward glance." Many people will tell you that I share this trait. I admit I do tend to have amnesia when it comes to bad news. I am sometimes called "Mr. Fantastic" because, no matter how bad a situation gets, when someone asks me how I'm doing I respond by saying, "Fantastic!" By refusing to dwell on negativity, I stay motivated and upbeat. I don't think this makes me a shallow or unrealistic person. Instead, I believe it makes me positive and committed.

DON'T FORGET TO LAUGH

Smiling is a start, but don't forget to follow that up with a hearty laugh. That goes for when times are both good and bad. Once, when I was feeling pretty sorry for myself because of a bad economy and some mistakes I had made, I said to my wife, "Honey, if I lost all of my money, do you think that you would still love me?" she paused, then looked up at me and said, "Of course I would love you, honey. I would miss you, but I would love you." I hadn't laughed that hard in a long time. A good laugh can really make your day and even help put your life into perspective.

I also stick my neck out quite a bit, sometimes with laughable results. One day I came home with a pair of rollerblades for both Rita and me. I was convinced that I could compete at the Olympian level someday (maybe inspired by my friend Vince, who you met earlier). Intent on trying to make this dream a reality, I hired a coach to help us, or me in particular, work on my technique and build speed. Every day, Rita and I would head out to some secluded area with our coach and try to advance our skills. After not too long, I developed some pretty major injuries. Finally, I decided to lay my ambition for an Olympic rollerblading medal to rest. So competitive rollerblading wasn't for me, at least I had tried it! And this time I made Rita laugh.

If I had been afraid of falling down, think of the fun I would have missed. Laugh in the face of failure whenever you can. The ability to laugh at yourself and at life is an amazing quality. No matter what changes are occurring in your life, laughter will help you move through them and profit from their lessons. Mark Twain once said, "Against the assault of laughter, nothing can stand."

I encourage you to pursue your potential. At best you'll succeed. At worst, you'll have stories to tell. Some failures may not seem so funny at the time, but the farther you move away from them, the more perspective you'll gain and the more you'll learn.

FOUNDATION 5:

REFLECTION

CHAPTER 17

LOOK BACK
TO MOVE AHEAD

Having first immigrated to Canada from England at age seven, I remember the sense of adventure in travelling to a new country. My favourite memory is of my mother and me standing on the deck of the *Queen Mary*, looking out at the ocean. The ship's motors churned up the water furiously, leaving behind a road of white wake. To my young eyes, that road appeared to stretch all the way to the horizon. I stood and stared, holding my mom's hand for what seemed like hours. I felt so confident in the future, so safe and secure, yet at the same time so full of trepidation—what would my new home look like, who would I meet, what new friends would I make? I still feel wonderful when I think back on that "best time."

You have probably experienced many best times like this in your life. Sometimes, a best time registers as an intense success; other times, it's a soft, quiet, warm glow, like a fire. The beauty of best times is that in difficult circumstances, you can quickly go to that place in your imagination.

In one particular bank meeting I attended when I was having serious financial challenges, the lawyers became particularly obnoxious so I let my mind drift back to the time I stood on the deck of the *Queen Mary* with my mom. I'm sure those lawyers were wondering why I sat there so calmly with a smile on my face. By recognizing and noticing best life experiences, reflecting on them and remembering them, you also gain strength and confidence to inspire you to greater heights. This is an important aspect of learning, growing, and continuing to succeed. Once you make this a habit, your self-esteem will grow and you'll attract more success into your life.

Reflecting on your best times and your successes is an important aspect of learning and growing. You'll gain the strength and confidence to inspire you to greater heights.

One night I was driving home from a very successful sales call in my 1963 Mercury S-55 convertible, with the radio blaring. I was on top of the world because not only did I make a sale to one family, they had invited their neighbours into their kitchen and I sold mutual funds to them, too! As I was driving, I wasn't thinking too much about the road or my speed—I was reflecting on my success.

All of a sudden, I heard the scream of sirens behind me. I pulled over and a tall policeman walked up to my window.

"Where do you think you're going in such a hurry?" he asked me.

Well, that was all the encouragement I needed. I had to tell him my good news and I did so with great excitement, talking 100 miles an hour like I'm known to do.

"I was on this sales call and, wouldn't you believe it, I didn't just sell one . . . "

He stopped me in the middle of my stream of talk.

"Go on, get out of here," he said.

I drove off, slightly slower, but still on top of the world. Even now, years later, when I'm in the middle of a deal, I frequently reflect back on that night with a smile.

"We often become so focused on our negatives that we lose sight of the positive aspects of ourselves," writes Gary Buffone in his book, *The Myth of Tomorrow*. "Our filter becomes clogged with negative thoughts, strangling the perceptions that encourage, support, and inspire our confidence." To feel good about ourselves, Buffone advises, "we must take time to appreciate our strengths and assets, and recognize what is working and going well in our lives. When time is short, gratitude grows. Our mortality begs us to be kind."

LOOK BACK TO SEE
HOW FAR YOU'VE COME

I like to tell the story of a farmer and his son in Saskatchewan who went out to the fields early one morning to take care of the crop. It was a huge field and the father gave his son instructions to use his pitchfork and make stooks of grain that he would gather with his threshing machine. The farmer then jumped on his tractor and took off.

After about two hours of non-stop work the farmer looked over at his son, who was standing still with his head down, sobbing, his fork still in his hands. The farmer got off the tractor, walked over to his son and asked, "Son, what's the matter?" The boy looked up, tears streaming down his cheeks, and pointed to what seemed like the endless field ahead that showed how much work he had left to do. The farmer took his son by the shoulder, turned him around and said, "But look how far you've come."

Like the farmer did for his son, I encourage you to reflect positively on what you've accomplished so far in your life.

RUMINATE OR REFLECT?

It is important to distinguish between ruminating and reflecting. An Ohio State University study shows there are two different types of self-analysis: self-rumination and self-reflection.

A person who engages in self-analysis is said to self-ruminate. That person questions how he or she looks and acts, and is often very insecure and lacking in confidence. It's "anxious attention," Alain Morin wrote in the *Science &*

Consciousness Review, "where the person is afraid to fail and keeps wondering about his/her self-worth."

A person who engages in self-reflection, on the other hand, is someone who is also highly self-aware, but instead of being anxious, feels secure and, Morin says, "philosophical about their shortcomings." He says self-reflection is "a genuine curiosity about the self, where the person is intrigued and interested in learning more about his or her emotions, values, thought processes, attitudes, etc."

As you begin to reflect, be careful not to ruminate, especially on parts of your past you may not be proud of. Instead of dwelling on the past, take what you've learned from it and apply it to the present and future. Also, don't rest on your laurels when it comes to good things you've done in your past. Value them, and build on them. Following this advice will help bring yourself closer to becoming the amazing person you were meant to be.

KEEP A RECORD OF YOUR LIFE

We all have bank records and keep track of our bills and other expenses, but what about a record of something even more important—your own life? A great way to remind yourself of the good times is to keep records of things that make you happy and proud. This includes keeping newspaper clippings, pictures and drawings, programs from hockey games or concerts and even business cards from your various jobs—anything that reminds you of feeling self-pride or simply having fun.

I also recommend that you write down your achievements to prove to yourself how many great things you have done in life so far. To do this, I suggest you start by finding some quiet time. Begin by writing down your successes from the past year. Don't just focus on career matters or how much money you've earned. Think about all aspects of your life.

One man who attended a LifePilot workshop thought he couldn't find any successes to reflect upon. His business was in deep trouble and that coloured his outlook. Encouraged to look deeper, he did acknowledge that he had learned to ride a horse that year. He also had been a good father. As well, he had started writing again and was enjoying it. In reflecting back, he realized he had been successful.

"The hardest arithmetic to master is that which enables us to count our blessings," writes Eric Hoffler in *Reflections on the Human Condition*. Too often we find it easier to think of blessings in the lives of other people. Ask yourself, "If I were a friend to myself, what would I view as successes in my life?" If you are still having trouble identifying your successes, ask people you like and trust to tell you what they think your successes have been.

UPDATE YOUR LIST

Don't write this success list just once. Keep at it. Set aside a regular time once a week, or if that seems too often, try on the same day of every month. Also, try to update your list when you are in a reflective mood. Sundays are often quiet, reflective days for many people. By adding to your list on a regular basis, you will be amazed at what you have accomplished. Reflecting on all of your successes, big and small, will help you begin to see accomplishments where you previously saw disappointments or setbacks. Your self-esteem will grow, which will help you attract more success into your life.

When I think of how important it is to keep a record of your life, I am reminded of the story of a family whose daughter was killed during the September 11, 2001 terrorist attacks while working in the World Trade Center. Her body was never found, but rescuers did recover from the rubble her laptop, which was returned to the family. The memory of losing their daughter was so painful that several years passed before they were able to turn on the computer and see what she had left behind. When they finally did, the family found among their daughter's documents a file called "Life List." On the list were one hundred things she had wanted to do during her lifetime. There were many things on that list that were checked off. In a media interview, the family commented on how much joy it brought them to know what her big dreams were and that she had achieved some of them.

191

CHAPTER 18

THE TOUCHSTONE FOR HEALTH AND HAPPINESS

I know many people who have extraordinary lives, but they just don't recognize it. They're always thinking about what they don't have, and forgetting about what they do have. They often search and search for what's missing in their lives, even when it's actually right there.

A story I like that brings this to mind is called "The Touchstone."

A young man was out walking when he meets an old wise man.

The wise man said, "If you can find a touchstone, I will buy it from you for one million dollars."

"Where can I find one of these stones?" the young man said.

"Oh, they are just lying on the beach," the wise man told him. "They look like any other stone, only they are almost too hot to touch. That's how you'll recognize one when you find it."

The man walked down to the beach and started sifting through the rocks in search of the touchstone. He did this for days, then months, then years. Eventually, he became a very old man. Even so, he went to the beach every day looking for a touchstone.

One day, as he was picking up stones and throwing them over his shoulder, he actually reached down and picked up a touchstone. He was so absorbed by throwing stones back in the water that he didn't notice the warmth of the touchstone. He just threw it over his shoulder and continued picking up stones and throwing them away. He had formed such a strong habit of tossing each pebble into the sea that, when the one he wanted came along, he threw it away like all the others.

So it is with the gifts in our lives. Sometimes we fail to recognize them and we miss what life is all about. We can throw our whole lives away looking for things we already have but don't treasure. Unless we are grateful for all we have, it is easy to overlook them when they are in hand and it is just as easy to toss them aside while we focus on what we believe we lack.

BE GRATEFUL

My friend Kevin Langley knows a lot about finding the gifts in life. Kevin, who is an executive in the construction business in New Orleans, lost his home and business as did thousands of others in August 2005 when Hurricane Katrina ripped through his city. "When I re-entered New Orleans in a boat and stood on the roof of my flooded, hurricane-ravaged house, I realized it was a tipping point in my life," Kevin recalls. "All of my neighbours and most of my employees lost their homes and everything in them. Several of our neighbours and friends, along with 1,836 other people, died from the hurricane-force winds and flooding alone."

But Kevin refuses to call himself a victim of Hurricane Katrina. Instead, he said the natural disaster tested his values, brought clarity and reminded him of the importance of community. "Somehow, what might have been a crippling blow to our morale and ability to function actually brought out the best," Kevin says. "It showed us, without question, that our future success is ultimately a result of our mindset and attitude. Katrina didn't cause the problems; it simply revealed them. Sometimes when we are in a comfort zone we miss the big picture. This disaster forced me to focus on what's important; family, friends, giving back, a sense of community."

Kevin has rebuilt his home and business and now helps entrepreneurs like him try to reach their full potential. For Kevin, that's one of the gifts he can give others.

"I realized that one of the great things about giving back to other entrepreneurs is that it really is a win/win situation," Kevin says. "We may be giving our time and talent, asking for nothing in return, but chances are, like it or not, we are going to receive much more benefit in unexpected ways as a result of our charitable actions. When you find clarity of purpose you can give it life and it will continue long after you are gone."

GAIN ENERGY FROM GRATITUDE

Researchers have found that when we think about someone or something we truly appreciate, and experience the feeling that goes with the thought, we trigger the parasympathetic or calming branch of the autonomic nervous system. With repetition, this pattern bestows a protective effect on the heart.

When you send out positive vibrations, you receive the same back from others. Showing gratitude passes positive energy from one person to another. It can positively affect someone's day, week or entire life. It also brings us happiness, which is healthy. Gratitude is a universal experience and has been a component of many religious traditions for centuries. Not only is it a desirable virtue, but an essential element to wholeness and well-being.

When I was a young man in the army I experienced an act of generosity that forever changed my life and how I treated other people. I was on a weekend pass when I decided to buy myself a used car. I saw a small black Austin that took my breath away. It was perfect. It had room for four, and it would be cheap to run. I decided to buy it, so I sat down with the manager to conduct my first meaningful transaction. The car cost $300 and I only had $50. "No problem," the manager told me. "Fifty dollars is enough to start." By then, I had all kinds of pictures in my head of me having fun with my new car. He brought out the papers for me to sign to borrow the other $250 from him. When it came time to sign, he asked me where I worked. I told him I was a soldier stationed at Camp Borden. At that point, his entire demeanour changed. He took the papers back. "I didn't know you were a soldier," he said. "I cannot offer you any financing." Naturally, I was distraught. Nothing I did or said changed his mind.

I left his office and hitchhiked right back to camp. I went into my barracks and sat on my bed. I must have looked very dejected because Duty Sergeant Jack Vart asked me why I was back at camp when I had a weekend pass. I told him the woeful story of the car. He left and came back a few minutes later. "I'm off duty," he said. "I'm driving back to Barrie so come on and we'll have a talk with the manager of the used car lot. I'll see if I can put in a good word for you."

At that point, I would have grasped at any straw. I thought I had exhausted every avenue, so I really had nothing to lose. When we got to the car lot, Sergeant Vart told me to wait in the car while he went in to talk to the manager. He returned to the car several minutes later and told me the man had changed his mind. I went in and the manager had all the papers ready to sign. "I'll make an exception in your case," he told me.

I drove that car for over a year and I cannot tell you how much happiness it brought me. One day after I had paid the car off, ahead of schedule, I received a letter and a copy of the agreement in the mail. When I read over the agreement, I saw there were actually two agreements. The first agreement had my signature on it, and the second one had the signature of Sergeant Vart. Until that moment, I had no idea he had actually provided his personal guarantee that I would pay for the car. He had assumed all the risk. I still get goosebumps thinking how he trusted me enough to put himself on the line for me. What's more, he didn't even tell me he had done it. I am forever grateful for Sergeant Vart's support. Today, if I can help someone through an act of trust, I do it. It just goes to show that you can change a life with an act of kindness.

WHO'S PACKING YOUR CHUTE?

There's a famous story about gratitude that involves Charles Plumb, a U.S. Naval Academy graduate, who was a jet fighter pilot in Vietnam. After seventy-five combat missions, his plane was destroyed by a surface-to-air missile. Plumb parachuted into enemy hands. He spent the next six years in a Vietnamese prison.

One day after the war was over, Plumb and his wife were sitting in a restaurant when a man at another table said, "You're Plumb! You flew jet fighters in Nam from the carrier *Kitty Hawk*. You were shot down!"

"How in the world did you know that?" asked Plumb.

"Oh, I was the one who packed your parachute," the man replied.

Plumb gasped in surprise and gratitude.

"Yep, I guess it worked!" the man laughed.

"It sure did work," Plumb said. "If your chute hadn't worked, I wouldn't be here today."

That night Plumb thought a lot about the man who had packed his parachute. He kept wondering what the man might have looked like in uniform.

"I wondered how many times I might have passed him on the *Kitty Hawk*. I wondered how many times I might have seen him and not even said 'good morning' or 'how are you?' or anything, because you see, I was a fighter pilot and he was just a sailor."

He thought of the many hours the man had spent at a long wooden table in the bowels of the ship, meticulously weaving the shrouds and folding the silks of each chute. Did he realize he held a man's life in his hands each time he packed one?

Plumb, now a motivational speaker, asks his audiences, "Who's packing your chute?" Showing appreciation, he feels, brings magic and blessings into the lives of those we meet.

How many times have we heard about people in the depths of despair who find their lives unexpectedly changed because of the kind words or acts of a stranger? What about people who felt inspired to achieve remarkable goals because a stranger showed appreciation?

As an unknown author wrote so poignantly, "To the world you may be just somebody, but to somebody you may just be the world."

HARNESS THE POWER OF APPRECIATION

Every human being needs to feel appreciated. Since we are unable to read each other's minds, as much as we would like to, we need to actively show people how much we appreciate them.

I learned a great lesson in the power of appreciation one year around Thanksgiving when I received a card from a fellow named Bill. The card said, "Dear Peter, I just want you to know that I appreciate having you in my life."

Receiving that card was one of the many moments in my life when I've felt truly humbled. I decided to pass that feeling on to others, so today I always carry notecards with me wherever I go. When I have a few spare moments, I'll write a note to someone I appreciate and mail it off. I truly believe that when you send out positive vibrations, you receive the same back from others.

Make a special effort to regularly say positive things to your friends, families, co-workers, clients and business associates—anyone in your life, really. Periodically review your experiences and identify people you admire. Write them letters expressing gratitude for what you've received from them. Be specific in your praise. Thank your customers by providing good service, kind words and thoughtful gifts, and they'll repay you with referrals. In appreciation for the good service you receive in a grocery store, dry cleaner or gas station, tell your friends about them so that their business can grow. To show your admiration to public servants and community activists, attend meetings and fundraisers, and volunteer to help.

SAY "THANK YOU"

"Thank you" are two of the most important but underused words in our language. Regardless of whether you verbalize them, write them or communicate them through tangible rewards, make a habit of using them to show your gratitude to people in your life. Words of encouragement offered at the right time can have a dramatic effect on people. Imagine how you feel when you receive a thank you from someone. Doesn't it bring a smile to your face, along with a sense of appreciation?

"Many people," writes Robert K. Cooper in *The Other 90%: How to Unlock Your Vast Untapped Potential for Leadership and Life*, "have come to tolerate the absence of respect and to expect poor recognition, or none at all, for the efforts they make. One of the main reasons why people end relationships in life or work is that they receive limited, if any, genuine praise or recognition for their contributions."

Saying thank you, according to motivational speaker Melody Beattie, "unlocks the fullness of life. It turns what we have into enough, and more. It turns denial into acceptance, chaos to order, and confusion to clarity. It can turn a meal into a feast, a house into a home, a stranger into a friend. Gratitude makes sense of our past, brings peace for today, and creates a vision for tomorrow."

Let people know you are thankful. After all, we all need to feel appreciated. And we are all interconnected, more than we might think.

An example of this is the story of a man who used to walk to work each morning past a jewellery shop that had a large clock in the window. The man always checked his watch against the clock. One day, as he was going to work, he did his usual stop and checked the clock. As he stood there, the owner of the shop came out and asked him why he looked in the window every morning. Was there something that he wanted to buy? The man said no, this was not the reason he stopped and looked into the window.

"I'm the person who blows the noon whistle in town each day," he told the shopkeeper. "Every morning I check my watch against the clock in the window to make sure my watch is correct."

The jeweller couldn't believe his ears. He said to the man, "I set my clock in the window each day by the noon whistle."

APPRECIATE YOURSELF

The only way to really appreciate others is to appreciate yourself first. To do this, try making a list of your strengths and positive qualities. Think about which aspects of your character really shine.

What positive things would others say about you? If you aren't sure, you may want to ask a few of the people who are closest to you about your best qualities. When you know your best qualities, you can play your best cards. You can also use this list to remind yourself of your value, instead of always relying on others for recognition.

Within each one of us there is a voice that says, "I am something special . . . I can make a difference . . . I have something to give to others." Listen to that voice. Honour that voice. Don't ever silence it or let it be silenced by anyone else.

CHAPTER 19

FIND YOUR SANCTUARY

There is a hundred-year-old limestone quarry in Victoria, British Columbia, that has been depleted of its stone. Many such quarries across Canada are thus—deserted and forgotten. Some are turned into swimming holes for the local kids. But this one is different because of the remarkable family who turned it into one of the world's most celebrated sunken gardens. Today, Butchart Gardens is a fifty-five-acre wonder, featuring flowers and plants from all over the world.

Overlooking the sunken garden is a spot where you can pause to drink in the garden's incredible beauty and serenity. No matter what is going on in my life, when I stand in this spot I feel inspired and connected to the beauty of Earth.

It is important to have your own personal sanctuary. We all need a place where we can go to reflect and feel inspired, reconnect with our inner selves and get away from life's everyday stresses. Your spot may not be a garden; it may be a riverbank, a beach, a mountaintop, a temple or a church, a café, or even a special place in your own home. Find your spot and try to spend a little time there when you can. It's good for your soul.

Even if you travel a lot, it's often not hard to find some personal space where you can relax, recharge and be inspired. One of the reasons I love to travel is because of the many different communities, cultures and landscapes that lie across this planet, from the big-city skyscrapers to the vast mountains, valleys and oceans. I have homes in a few different places, and each one I chose because of its unique characteristics. Victoria has the ocean, Arizona the desert and Switzerland the mountains. Each of these areas, where humans have carved out their own little islands, is humbled by the gigantic forces of nature that surround them, such as sand storms, tidal waves or avalanches. When I am reminded of these forces, any challenges I may have in life suddenly seem pretty insignificant. This inspires me. It makes me believe that anything is possible.

When searching for your sanctuary, I suggest you look for a place that allows you to feel creative, and helps you think and believe that your dreams can become a reality. Here are a few thoughts to consider when finding your personal sanctuary:

FIX YOUR SPACE IN YOUR MIND

Consider what your requirements are to truly relax, from size to what you need in the space. If it's a sanctuary away from home, such as a garden, or your favourite neighbour-hood coffee shop, consider what you need to bring with you to enjoy your relaxation time. Maybe it's your iPod, a news-paper or a notebook. If it's a home sanctuary, do you need your own special room? Maybe it's just your favourite couch or a table and chair in a room full of plants. Find what works best for you.

TAKE IN THE SOUND OF MUSIC

I have already told you about my love of music, so it's no sur-prise that I would recommend adding a little sound to your sanctuary. It doesn't have to be your favourite country singer or a song from your youth. In a sanctuary, the sound of fall-ing water might work best for you.

You can also make any space your sanctuary with music. If you are on a crowded bus, in a lineup or on a long flight, pop on a set of headphones, press "play," close your eyes and in seconds you can be anywhere you want.

COLOUR YOUR WORLD

Many people overlook the power of colour to change your mood. The right colours soothe and relax; the wrong colours add stress. Colours can affect and recharge every cell of your body. That's why it's important to consider colour in your personal sanctuary.

Pick a colour that inspires you, that makes you feel calm and happy. Many experts believe the colour green is great for relaxation because it mimics nature's own resplendent hue. Blues, pale pink, and lavender are also soothing for some.

ENJOY THE SWEET SMELL OF AROMATHERAPY

Certain smells can help clear the mind, balance emotions and boost confidence. There are also scents, such as freshly baked bread, a cup of coffee, or a garden after rain, that bring back fond memories. The trick is to find the smell that tweaks your positives senses. Seek out smells that you find soothing and use them to stir creativity and help you relax.

Remember that your sanctuary, no matter what or where it is, should be an atmosphere that inspires you and helps you focus and visualize your goals and dreams. It should be a place where you can reflect and feel like your true self.

As author Christopher Forrest McDowell said, "Sanctuary, on a personal level, is where we perform the job of taking care of our soul."

CHAPTER 20

YOUR LIFE CAN BE
WHAT YOU WANT IT TO BE

I often reflect on the unexpected turns my life has taken. I've had many successes and overcome my share of obstacles. I was sixty years old when I had to completely turn my life around, personally and emotionally, after the death of my only son. I also have been both financially rich and in the red. The trials, triumphs and challenges of my past have shaped me into a very different person—a better person, I believe. I have learned to develop my strengths and work on my weaknesses instead of using them as excuses.

How blessed am I? Very. I believe part of what makes me blessed is the ability to embrace change and be open to personal growth. I wish someone had told me earlier about the importance of values, and how they can simplify and amplify our lives. But I also believe strongly that it's never too late to define your values and use them to guide you to a better life. In my workshops, I have seen the power that recognizing your values can have for people of all ages, races and religions. As the old saying goes, "It's never too late to make a new beginning."

My goal with this book has been to show you how to live life according to your values. That doesn't necessarily mean turning your life upside down, unless of course that's what you want. The real change first has to come from within. It is vital to develop a strong sense of who you are and what you want to accomplish in life. That's where defining your values comes in. Once you've done that, stay true to yourself, no matter what your obstacles, and turn your obstacles into opportunities.

I've tried always to instill in people this message:

Your life can be what you want it to be.

You can do whatever you want to do.

You don't have to take no, or rejection, for an answer.

You don't have to settle.

You have an obligation to yourself to create an extraordinary life.

The time to do that is now.

It's also important be realistic about how long it may take to succeed. As I said in the introduction to this book, there's no deadline. Remember, too, that success is not necessarily about making money. To me, success is achieving any goal you set for yourself. That can include anything from being a great parent to losing weight, giving more back to your community or being good at your job.

As I've said many times now, if you stick to your values, life becomes easier. That's my mantra. I believe it so strongly that I can't help but spread the message. It's now my life's work. When you begin to live your life aligned with your values, you will understand exactly what I mean. The process has worked for me, as well as many others who have joined me on this life-changing journey.

Thank you for taking the time to read about and share my life experiences. I hope this book has been an inspiration to you. I would like to leave you with this poem I wrote, which I believe can help you truly be great:

Keep your thoughts positive
Because your thoughts become your words.
Keep your words positive
Because your words become your actions.
Keep your actions positive
Because your actions become your values.
Keep your values positive
Because your values become your destiny.

～